# MAKING CONTACT

# MAKING

Arthur C. Wassmer, Ph.D.

# CONTACT

*A Guide to Overcoming Shyness,
Making New Relationships, and
Keeping Those You Already Have*

**THE DIAL PRESS**
**NEW YORK**

Published by
The Dial Press
1 Dag Hammarskjold Plaza
New York, New York 10017
by arrangement with Sayre Ross

Manufactured in the United States of America

First printing

**Library of Congress Cataloging in Publication Data**

Wassmer, Arthur C
  Making contact.

  1. Interpersonal relations.   2. Bashfulness.
3. Interpersonal communication.   I. Title.
HM132.W33     158'.2     78-17692
ISBN 0-8037-6283-6

*For Holly and April,*
*who taught me how shyness feels*
*to the one who experiences it*

# Contents

*Contents*

# Introduction

SHYNESS MAY BE at once the most widespread and the least noticed psychological problem of Americans today. As a people, we are known throughout the world as affluent, efficient, and confident. It seems somehow shameful to us that, as research has indicated, forty percent or more of us experience shyness as a serious problem in our personal lives.

Perhaps it is the very ease of our personal lives that spoils us when it comes to taking care of ourselves emotionally and interpersonally. In a society of goods and services, we are often at a loss as to how to develop the ease of human contact that is more precious than money can buy. Every night in our cities and towns people walk the streets and stalk the bars, hoping by chance to satisfy their craving for personal closeness. Massage parlors and "adult communication centers" do a thriving business providing the illusion of a loving touch. Bars are filled from wall to wall with strikingly beautiful people trying to appear absorbed in music and drinks while hoping deep inside that some braver, more skillful person will somehow reach out and touch their spirit.

Shy people are not only the single, the unattached, the newly widowed, or divorced. They are young, old, city dwellers, and rural folk. Shy people are a group, perhaps even a majority of people, in every social class and category. Shy people are those who feel a tension, anxiety, or inhibition that gets in the way of making genuine human contact with other people. They are people, like you and me, who want more—more depth, more honesty, more meaning in their contact with others—but who get less, and feel lonely and cheated by the barrier within themselves that isolates them from other people.

There is good news for shy people. Relatively recent developments in the field of psychology show us that there are some specific things people can do to promote more meaningful relationships. Not only have these things been identified, but we now know for certain that they can be taught and they can be learned. Thus far, however, these techniques have been used mainly in the training of counselors and psychologists. In this book, many of the same methods used by professionals to establish good relationships with their patients will be made available to you to help overcome your shyness.

My doctoral research was devoted to the study of methods for training counselors. Although much of the work was very complex, the most important thing I found was quite simple—good counselors are trained, not born. Research had found ways to train people to establish warm and helpful relationships with others in a very short period of time.

I wondered whether these same training methods could be applied to shy people. To explore this question, I began to experiment with "training" some of my shy patients in exactly the same ways I had been training my students in counseling. Not every patient, of course, was successful in overcoming shyness completely, but I found that those who were willing to believe that their problem had a solution, and who followed the simple directions found in this book, achieved significant, and in some cases, radical improvement in the depth, meaning, spontaneity, and joy in their relationships.

I'm hopeful that the same will happen for you. The first section of this book tells you the steps you can take to change your thoughts, feelings, and attitudes in ways that will lead to more satisfying and enjoyable interpersonal contact. The second section presents some technical skills that you'll find quite easy to master with a little practice and will start you on your way to actively reaching out to make contact. The third section discusses some specific areas of life where you will want to use your new skills.

Try using the exercises provided at the end of many of the chapters. We are, after all, talking about changing the way you behave in the direction of becoming more "contact effective." You wouldn't expect to become a better skier just by reading a book about ski techniques and not practicing those techniques on the slopes. In the same way, getting better at making contact takes a little practice. I believe that you will find even the practice exciting and rewarding.

I wish you all the joy that comes with discovering the warmth of making contact with others.

# MAKING CONTACT

# ONE

# The Anatomy of Shyness

THE ROOTS OF SHYNESS are negative thoughts that people hold about themselves. Those negative thoughts interrupt their contact with others and cause it to fail. Although the roots remain the same in almost every case, people express their shyness in many different ways.

Julie is a twenty-two-year-old graduate student who was almost unable to say anything in a group of more than three people. "Every time the conversation comes around to me," she said, "I just don't know what to say. I feel like everyone's looking at me, waiting for me to say something worth hearing, and I kind of freeze up."

Alan is a twenty-nine-year-old junior executive whose wife recently divorced him. When he began to date again, he found himself paralyzed around women. "As soon as we're alone, I try to think of appropriate things to say, but I never get much further than the weather. I start wondering how I got myself into this mess, and all I want to do is get out. But next week I go and do it all over again."

Terry is a thirty-six-year-old engineer. He has been
married for twelve years, has three children, and a
home in the suburbs. He feels that his marriage is
dying on the vine, not for lack of love, but from
boredom. "We just don't have anything to say to each
other. Sure I have thoughts and feelings, and I'm sure
she does too, but how can you talk about all that?
Mostly we watch TV, even though neither of us really wants to. I guess it's the easy way out."

Kim is sixteen. She is very attractive high school
junior, a straight-A student. She says, "Everybody at
school thinks I'm stuck up. Somehow, whenever any-
body talks to me, I get scared. I never know what to
say. Sometimes I pretend I didn't hear them, and go
about my business. I just wish I had some friends!"

Each of these very different people feels somehow
inadequate. And the pattern is usually the same—the
person starts out with a set of negative ideas about
himself or herself. This self-image (or self-concept) produces certain kinds of behavior, especially in contact
with others, that are also negative and unhelpful. As a
result, contacts with other persons fail, and that failure
serves to emphasize and reinforce one's negative self-
image.

Of course, nobody likes to be a failure. It doesn't take
too many uncomfortable social situations to teach us to
avoid circumstances where we might fail. Unfortunately, avoiding social situations cuts us off from opportunities to learn other, more effective ways to relate to
people.

There are many kinds of negative self-images. But

basically, all people with a negative self-image feel that they are different from or inferior to other people. Only the reasons are different. "I'm fat," one person says. "I'm not intelligent," says another. "I just don't know how to do anything," says a third. "I come from the wrong side of the tracks," says still another.

Many people can't even give a specific reason. "I just feel deep down," said one client to me, "that I'm not like other people. It's as if they were born with something I wasn't. It's like there's something missing, and if I had it, I'd be all right."

These feelings about ourselves are not just incidental emotions. They affect our attitudes and behavior in every aspect of life. In contacts with others we feel "one down"—as if, somehow, the other persons are "okay" and we are not. Like Charlie Brown in the comic strip, we feel that other people are *always* heroes, while we are *always* goats. These negative thoughts become firmly established in the mind and become what psychiatrist Thomas Harris calls a "life position," the point of view from which we see the world.

We all form our attitudes and pattern our behavior not only on fact, but also on what we believe to be true. Columbus dared to sail across the ocean because he believed that the world was round. Others of his time feared to undertake such a voyage because they believed that the world was flat and that they would fall off its edge. I roll on the floor and wrestle with my 150-pound dog because I believe he likes me and will not injure me. I have a friend, however, who prefers that I put the dog out while he is in my home because he has the idea that large dogs are fearsome, vicious beasts who are likely to attack him. When you carry your umbrella to work in the morning, you do so because you believe it might rain. If you think the day will be sunny, you leave the umbrella at home. We act, all of us, in accordance with the ideas and beliefs we have about the way things are. So if you think you are different or inferior, then you will act as if you are, and that's how other people will come to see you.

The behavior of persons who think they are different and inferior falls into some rather easily identified patterns. The first of these is the tendency to respond to social situations with anxiety or psychological fear. Even when you're not aware of feeling afraid in the presence of others, your body often gives you signs that you are feeling anxious. The typical anxiety reaction involves an increase in the heartbeat rate, often accompanied by the feeling that your heart is "pounding." Sweating, blushing, butterflies in the stomach, roaring in the ears and, in some extreme cases, a feeling of being "far away," are all common physical signs of anxiety.

This anxiety leads quite naturally to a second characteristic, the tendency toward *self-consciousness* rather than *other-consciousness*. With anxiety threatening to overwhelm you, your attention focuses on the turmoil going on within, rather than on the person you are with. Part of this self-concern is an attempt to control your anxiety. You struggle to stop your voice from shaking, calm your trembling hands, and keep yourself under control. But with the focus of attention so powerfully drawn inward, you often fail to hear accurately what others are saying, let alone really make contact with them.

When shy persons become caught up in this deadly combination of anxiety and self-consciousness, they begin to withdraw. More and more, they lose contact with the discussion going on. Other people see or feel their discomfort, but most often they don't understand it. People who are less sensitive may conclude that the shy person is bored, unfriendly, hostile, or superior (this is how a painfully shy high-school student may get branded with the label "stuck up"). Believing themselves to be rejected, they withdraw from contact, leaving the shy person even more isolated.

People who are more sensitive to shy persons are not misled about their discomfort—they just don't know what to do about it. They try to ignore the sweating palms, the trembling voice, and the silence. They don't understand when the shy person's embarrassment is even further increased by their indulgence. They try in a friendly manner to draw the person out, and then feel futile and confused when the person reacts to their questions by retreating even deeper. In the end, sadly, they also withdraw from the person, feeling frustrated and unable to help.

The very unfunny irony about these kinds of situations is that both parties end up feeling rejected. The people who try to make contact with the shy person feel rejected because their best approach got no response. The shy person feels rejected because the other person or persons ended up withdrawing. Even more unfortunately, shy persons usually mistake the withdrawal of others as confirmation of their negative self-image ("See, I told you they wouldn't like me!"). It's another failure and they hoped it would not happen—but they knew "in their hearts" that it would.

It requires surprisingly few of these painful episodes to produce what psychologists call a "conditioned response." It was the Russian scientist Ivan Pavlov who opened the doors for the discovery that behavior is learned according to the principle of reinforcement. Simply stated, the principle says that an action that results in pleasure will tend to be repeated in the future, while an action that results in pain will tend to be avoided. The shy person's behavior is a great example of this theory. A certain kind of social situation goes wrong a few times, causing a fair amount of pain or embarrassment. The next time that situation comes up, the shy person's first thought is how to avoid the situation. The fear of failing again causes the butterflies to flutter and the muscles to tighten, and all the shy one wants is to escape. A shy person learns to avoid such painful situations as surely as a child learns not to touch a hot stove. After one or two painful experiences, the socially burned person begins to develop all sorts of dodges to avoid the hot plate of social contact.

One of the most common of these dodges is what I call the wallflower syndrome. That quaint old term "wallflower" first applied to the shy young man or woman who seemed to melt into the floral print of the wallpaper in a Victorian drawing room. The person was there, but was somehow never noticed. Shy persons of today place the same importance on being invisible and on maintaining a "low profile." They desire not to be noticed for fear attention will draw them into contact with others. They move slowly, speak quietly and, above all, avoid doing anything that might attract attention.

The wallflower also develops some nonverbal signals, or "body language," that effectively communicate a desire to be left alone. The most prominent of these is the avoidance of eye contact. Our shy friend has learned that if you consistently meet a person's eyes, sooner or later he or she will speak to you. The shy one avoids the other person's eyes and thus greatly reduces the chances of being drawn into a conversation. Shy people also tend to maintain a "closed posture"—arms or legs crossed—indicating unwillingness to meet or be close to others. To other people the shy person appears to be unapproachable.

The wallflower syndrome is, of course, highly effective in discouraging contact. If another person ignores these obstacles and starts a conversation, the shy person will discourage it in a hurry. He or she is a master of the one-word answer. Consider this example:

"Are you from Seattle?" (Questioner smiles, looks interested.)

"Yes." (Wallflower looks away, crosses arms, looks uncomfortable.)

"Oh. Uh, it's a nice party, isn't it?" (Questioner smiles hopefully, leans forward.)

"I guess so." (Wallflower is really uncomfortable now, getting panicky. Stares intently at a picture on the wall, squirms a bit, thinks, "Oh God, let me think of something to say.")

"Mm-hm. Well, uh, do you work here in town?"

(Questioner wonders how he ever got into this. Feels wallflower's discomfort, doesn't understand.)

"Yes." ("What a klutz I am," wallflower thinks. "Why wasn't I born witty, or intelligent, or companionable?")

"Yeah. Well, I see old Charley over there. If you'll excuse me, I think I'll go over and touch bases with him." ("Whew!" thinks questioner. "Let me step into the bathroom and check if my mouthwash and deodorant are still working.")

"Sure." ("Well, I knew it," thinks the shy one. "I'm just a social retard. I'm so dumb I can't even think of something to say. I hate parties!")

If all other methods of avoiding contact fail, severely shy persons may even develop some forms of psychosomatic illness. Headaches, nausea, diarrhea, cramps, dizziness, flushing, and even fever can be brought on by extreme anxiety. For some socially inadequate folks the illness is its own cure, since it enables them to avoid situations in which they might risk having to meet and deal with others.

What I have said so far may create the impression that shy persons do not want and hope for truly meaningful relationships with others. This is emphatically not the case. Incidents of interpersonal failure and their accompanying pain have taught shy persons to avoid any real contact with others, but that does not alter the fact that they both need and want it. In fact, the very absence of deep, meaningful relationships in such a person's life makes the ideal of genuine contact all the more precious.

As Dr. Phillip Zimbardo suggests in an article on

shyness in *Psychology Today* (May 1975), "Shyness becomes a form of imprisonment in which the person plays both the role of guard, who constantly enforces restrictive rules, and the role of prisoner, who sheepishly follows them and thus earns the contempt of the guard." Shy people actually hide in their own jails, imprisoned by fear of failure, rejection, embarrassment, and anxiety. They hope someone will come and help them get out, but if anyone comes near, the "guard" shouts, "Stay away, this person is no good." And the jail cell does have its advantages. It is safe. It does protect one from failure and disappointment. But the disadvantages are overwhelming. It's a place of bread and water. It's lonely, isolated, and bare, and not a pleasant place for work, marriage, sexual experience, or social relationships.

The picture of the shy person I have presented here is extreme. Seldom are all of the thoughts, feelings, and behaviors I've described found in one person. Many shy people have positive as well as negative beliefs about themselves. Some have only moderate feelings of discomfort in social situations. Some manage to disguise their shyness so that other people do not identify them as shy at all. But the fact remains: For many, shyness is a serious and unhappy condition that keeps them from realizing their own potential and limits their ability to make satisfying contact with other people.

The important truth is that no matter how often or how severely you experience shyness, you can change. The key to the door of your cell is in your hands. Unlocking the door begins with your personal commitment to change. The suggestions and exercises pre-

sented in the following chapters depend for their use-
fulness on your desire to give up the ineffective patterns of behavior you have followed in the past. You
must really want enjoyment in your relationships with
others. Having made the commitment, you can begin
to overcome your shyness one step at a time. It will
take a bit of daring—some of the new ways of thinking and acting may seem strange and uncomfortable
at first. But these new ways are really stepping-stones
to the warm, exciting, and rewarding world of deep
and meaningful contact with others.

*TWO*

# How Did I Get Here?

WHEN YOU FIND YOURSELF in an unpleasant place, such as a social situation where the possibility of contact with others brings on negative thoughts about yourself, anxiety, and a general sense of loneliness, you are likely to ask, "How did I get here?"

"How did I get here?" the subject of this chapter, is an important question because one of the ways to leave an unpleasant situation is to retrace your steps, the way Hansel and Gretel did in the fairy tale. You may also find out where you made the wrong turn in the first place—the turn that led to your sense of failure and discomfort. The early psychoanalysts believed that if you could retrace your development and find out how you got to be the way you are, your problem would be solved. Unfortunately, simply understanding a problem doesn't necessarily solve it. On the other hand, a problem that's fully understood may be a lot easier to solve than one that's not.

A somewhat newer school of psychological thought, known as behaviorism, maintains that the "how did I get here" question isn't important at all. What is impor-

**13**

2 truth-
objective
subjective

tant, this school contends, is the question, "Where can I go from here?" The behaviorist's emphasis on taking immediate action suggests a more direct path to solving personal problems than the psychoanalyst's years of study of the deep subconscious. But behaviorism has often been too optimistic and has failed to give troubled persons a sufficiently clear sense of direction. Like the stranger trying to follow the complex directions given by a local resident, the troubled person often doesn't know how to follow the behaviorist's advice even when the advice is correct.

We will be drawing on the thoughts of both psychoanalysts and behaviorists in this book in the belief that a combination of their insights is the best way of explaining and helping shyness. In this chapter we are asking, with the psychoanalysts, how the shy person got the way he or she is. Even if you can find all the right answers to this question after reading this chapter, your shyness will not be cured. But by understanding yourself better, you will be more ready to take action. In fact, people often find a sense of hope in studying their own life histories. Many come to believe for the first time that their problems really can be solved and that they really can learn to lead happier lives.

In Chapter 1 we concluded that shy persons have negative and unhelpful ideas about themselves—a negative self-image. We build our self-image out of two different kinds of truth. The first kind is _objective truths, or facts._ These are statements that can be confirmed by physical or historical examination. If you ask me to tell you who I am, I can give you an answer consisting entirely of objective truths. I was born in

Newark, New Jersey. I have worked as a truck driver, a clothing salesman, a schoolteacher, a social worker, and a psychologist. I attended school and received the B.A., M.A., and Ph.D. degrees. I now live in Kirkland, Washington. All these facts could be verified by anyone who wanted to spend a week or two inquiring of the proper authorities.

A second order of truths, however, plays a far greater role in determining a person's self-image and therefore his or her individual style of behavior. These are known as subjective truths, because their ultimate truth or falsity depends wholly on the person whose truths they are. The state of your feelings, your attitude toward yourself, and the personality characteristics you see in yourself are all subjective truths.

Subjective truths are arrived at indirectly. They require not only observation or memory but also evaluations, judgments, and conclusions. When I give you a self-description consisting primarily of subjective truths, you get a better idea of what it feels like to be me. I am reasonably happy, I may say, though some of my hopes and ambitions remain to be fulfilled. I am generally outgoing, talkative, confident, and even a bit aggressive. I have always felt that I am too short and too fat.

While objective truths can be confirmed or proved wrong, subjective truths are true only because you (or I), the experiencing subject, feel that they are true. I may tell you that I have always felt I was too short, but I haven't told you whether I am 5-foot-2 or 6-foot-1, too short to get into the Army or too short to play professional basketball. Subjective truths are based on my feelings. They are my evaluations of the way things are.

Subjective truths are very complicated even when they seem simple. When I tell you that I am a reasonably happy person, I am not indicating which specific experiences this conclusion was drawn from. I give the impression that this relative happiness is something I was born with, that it is a permanent character trait. But what I am really saying is that I have had enough happy experiences to keep me optimistic about myself and my life. As these experiences mounted up, it became too complicated to maintain a running tally of "happy" against "unhappy" experiences. So for convenience' sake, I formed a conclusion about my experiences as a whole and concluded that I am a reasonably happy person.

Once I reach such a conclusion and establish it as a subjective truth, I tend to "close the file" on that conclusion and to ignore any new experiences that might change my mind. The conclusion lies in the archives of my subconscious mind, more or less protected from the impact of any new experiences that may change or question it. It has become a part of my self-image. Having once concluded that I am a relatively happy person, I can experience quite a number of unhappy events without ever changing that subjective truth.

One famous theorist of personality, Alfred Adler, called these subjective truths "fictional finalisms." They're fictional because they were based on a fairly small number of experiences, yet are used as if they were a general truth. The conclusions are final because they have been "filed away" in the subconscious and are extremely resistant to change by later experiences.

So when people come to my office and begin to describe their personalities to me, I understand them to be telling me what subjective truths they have accepted about themselves. In my experience it is quite rare for persons to be aware at first of how they became shy, withdrawn, or "unpopular," because the subjective truth has been formed subconsciously. When I encourage people to explore the experiences that produced their idea of themselves, they are usually surprised and delighted to discover that the subjective truths they have formed about themselves are not attached to them in the same way as an arm or a leg. A real sense of freedom comes when they realize that subjective truths can be changed. Unhappy people can become happy and shy people unshy. Shyness is not an unchangeable part of your personality.

## Where Did Your Self-Image Come From?

Everyone begins forming a self-impression and impressions of other people and the world in general shortly after birth. In fact, the first year or two of life is very important in determining what kind of self-image we will develop. Since we have neither language nor prior experience nor the power of complex thought to weigh and judge our early experiences, we consider whatever happens to us as normal. Almost all of our contact is with our mothers or fathers. They are the first "sample" on which we decide what the world is like. We form vague, symbolic, and extremely general subjective truths about ourselves, other people, and the world based on small and seemingly insignificant experiences.

If our mother had little milk or a nipple that was hard to draw from, we may come to feel that other people don't have much nurturance to offer us. If our parents were given to shouting and violence, we may conclude that the world is a violent, unstable place. Falling from a parent's arms can lead to the generalization that other people are not to be trusted. The experience of being momentarily smothered by a breast or body may result in a fear of physical closeness. Yet for all the strength of the truths formed during this period, it is difficult or even impossible to trace our conclusions back to the particular event or series of events. Fortunately, while it is helpful to know how our early subjective truths originated, this knowledge is not necessary in order for the truths to be modified.

Early childhood, from ages two to five, is another important period for the development of subjective truths. At this stage we begin to be active participants in our growth, trying to achieve a certain kind of relationship with our parents and others. Consistent responses of "not now, I'm busy" may create the subjective impression that our concerns are not important to others. The old chestnut that "children should be seen and not heard" may translate to the subjective truth that other people don't want to hear what we have to say. Differences between the mother's and father's way of relating to us may develop subjective truths about our role as boys (men) or girls (women). Whether or not physical contact is encouraged by our parents will give us subjective truths about our own bodies and the worth of physical intimacy. The kinds of conditioning we receive in these early years are very often reinforced by our parents for many years afterward, so it's often difficult to know how far back we first came to a conclusion about the way we are.

Consider the following example:

> David is a thirty-six-year-old electronics engineer who came for help when his wife threatened to leave him because he was such a cold fish. She complained that, although he was an excellent provider and a faithful spouse, in nine years of marriage she had never had a really clear idea of his emotional response to anything. He never seemed angry. He never got excited. He never felt depressed. Worst of all, he never expressed any particularly warm affection for her. David expressed his subjective truth on the subject when he said, "It's not that I don't have feelings—in fact, I think I may be too emotional a person. But I can't articulate those feelings. It's just that when I start to talk about a feeling, either it's not there any more, or I get choked up and uncomfortable. So it just makes more sense not to try."

We began to explore the kinds of experiences from which David had formed his self-label of "emotionally unexpressive." Because this behavior was spread rather evenly over all his interactions with people, rather than occurring in just one kind of situation, I suspected that David's subjective label was the product of conditioning from a very early age. It turned out that both of his parents were extremely unexpressive people. He had never seen either of them cry, shout, or kiss each other. The most descriptive adjectives he could find to portray his parents' personalities to me were "successful and

highly principled" for his father, and "proper—a real
lady" for his mother. He recalled that once, when he
was ten, his father had taken him on a hunting trip.
While walking along a trail, David fell, bruising his
elbow on a stone. He ran crying to his father, who
turned away with an expression of disgust, and said, "I
thought I was raising a man, but I guess all I've got is
a baby." David could never recall crying after this incident. As we talked further, he recalled an earlier episode in which he had come running from his playroom
and thrown his arms around his mother's neck, kissed
her, and said, "I love you, mommy." Mother, he
remembered clearly, had flushed deeply, disengaged
herself from David's arms, and replied, "Yes, dear, of
course you do. We're all very fond of each other in our
family." There were many more of these kinds of inter-
changes which, though no one of them could readily be
called traumatic, had, in their total impact, trained
David to believe that any genuine expression of feeling
would result in a painful experience of embarrassment
and rejection.

David gradually came to see that his emotionless behavior, and the subjective truth that the world would
punish a show of feelings, were the product of his parents' early training. He realized that these "lessons"
had been taught by only two teachers and that they
might not reflect the world as others experienced it.
Slowly, with the aid of exercises designed to help him
state his feelings, he was able to introduce a climate of
warmer feeling. Though he never became a walking
whirlwind of emotion, the hoped-for result of therapy
was achieved—his marriage remained intact and grew
in depth and meaning.

David wrote me several months after therapy was finished and said that his new freedom affected all areas of his life. "The feeling that I am ultimately alone with my inner thoughts and feelings, an emotional island unto myself, is gone. I've replaced it with the knowledge that I can 'make contact' with others when and to the extent that I want to, if I will swallow the fears from my past and let others know what I'm thinking and feeling."

The day we enter school marks the beginning of a whole new chapter in our development. Entirely new issues in our relationships with others are raised. We are exposed, for the first time, to a relatively large group of children our own age, and we are expected to work out some way of getting along with them. At the same time, we must find a way to relate successfully to the teacher, an adult in a position of authority who does not have the same taken-for-granted investment in us as our parents. To further complicate matters, we are asked to perform intellectually, which constitutes the first real task demanded of us other than to "be good." It's also our first step into the ratings game. The climate of emotional upheaval and change makes this a prime time for the learning of new subjective truths and the reinforcement of old ones.

There's an almost endless list of negative subjective truths that can be formed during the early school years. The very common experience of soiling one's pants on the first day of school can lead an individual to feel permanently that "I can't control myself." Experiencing the tactless and sometimes cruel responses of the other kids to some outstanding physical difference, such as thick glasses, fatness, or even funny clothes, may

cause a child to feel that relating to others will only lead to being made fun of. An immediate and very harsh crackdown by the teacher on some childish prank may lead the individual to define anyone in authority as "the enemy," leaving him unable to relate effectively to authority figures in later life. An illness causing absences during the first few weeks of school can lead a child to see himself as an outsider, and later to believe that he can't compete or keep up intellectually.

The next predictably violent storm of subjective truth-making comes with the onslaught of adolescence. We suddenly discover the "pain and delight," in Verdi's words, of the opposite sex. Group popularity becomes an even more important issue than before. The terrifying task of learning "the social graces"—how to eat in public, how to dance, how to talk to someone of the opposite sex—looms large before us. To make matters worse, our bodies are doing the strangest things at the most amazing rate. He's growing a beard, she's growing breasts. He's added five inches to his height and four shoe sizes this year, and is trying to learn how to make them all move at the same time, in the proper direction.

Our experiences at this time, of course, contribute immensely to the development of our concepts of ourselves as social and sexual beings. Am I popular or unpopular? Am I attractive (able to arouse interest in the opposite sex through my appearance) or unattractive? Can I trust myself to say and do the right things at the right time, or must I be afraid that every time I open my mouth I'll put my foot in it? Many of the subjective truths people will keep about themselves are formed by

this time. However, the mental file is still open, and bad experiences will tend to make the final self-label fall more in a negative direction.

> Daisy was a twenty-four-year-old graduate student in sociology who complained of a panicky inability to speak when she was in a group of more than three people. Often, because she was so silent in these groups, someone would ask her a direct question in the hope of drawing her into the conversation. When this happened, her eyes would grow large with fear, her skin would flush and sweat, and she would try to speak, only to find her voice blocked with a painful lump in her throat. She had been successfully avoiding group situations for years, but now she was enrolled in a small graduate seminar that required individual participation from each student. She expressed the subjective truth about herself as, "I'm just not able to speak in a group." At the point when she came for therapy, she was actively considering dropping out of grad school in order to avoid this situation, even though she was maintaining a near-perfect grade point average.

I explained to Daisy that even though she felt as if it were an absolute truth that she was not a group speaker, this feeling was a conclusion she had formed from an experience, or a set of experiences; she had filed it away in her subconscious and had never really bothered to question it ever since. We began to explore some of the experiences she had had with being asked to speak in a group situation. After several sessions she recalled one that she had not thought of for years.

When she was a freshman in high school, Daisy had a terrific crush on the boy who sat in front of her in chemistry class. One day she came to school fighting off a powerful attack of the flu. In chem class that day she was asked a question by the teacher. As she opened her mouth to reply, she was seized by a violent surge of nausea, and without warning vomited all over the boy in front of her. Mortified, she ran crying from the class, stayed home for a week, and was persuaded only by the strongest of threats from her parents even to go back to school at all.

It seemed clear that Daisy's public speaking behavior was rooted in a fear of getting into any situation that was even vaguely similar to her awful high school experience. As we discussed the episode, Daisy realized that what had happened was perfectly natural and outside her control, even though it was unfortunate and certainly embarrassing. She finally was able to separate the incident from her identity. It would be a nice conclusion to the story to be able to say that her difficulty magically disappeared with the insight, but this was not the case. There was an advantage gained by "reopening her file" on this particular subjective truth, however. She was able, under supervised conditions, slowly to add more positive group-speaking experiences to the file. Daisy never became a second Clarence Darrow, but she was able to modify her self-label to the extent that she felt reasonably comfortable about speaking to a small group.

Even our experiences in young adulthood, to the extent that they open new files of experience, can contribute to a self-concept. During this period we form a picture of ourselves as relationship partners and as participants in the world of work. By this time, of course, most experiences are merely extensions or logical outcomes of our already established self-truths. But occasional dramatic changes in our experience may open entirely new files that can change old self-truths or establish new ones. A sudden change in vocational status, winning the Irish Sweepstakes, beginning a romantic relationship with someone unlike anyone we have known before may lead to the development of new subjective truths.

Discovering the source and content of our self-concepts is important because the subjective truths we hold, whether consciously or subconsciously, are the single most important factor in determining our behavior. We act as if we are the individuals we believe ourselves to be, and as if the world is the place we believe it to be. If I believe that the world offers warmth, comfort, and love, I will behave in a manner that reaches out and seeks these things, and therefore I will find them. If I believe that I am physically attractive, then I will be sensitive to and aware of the attraction that others feel to me. If I believe that I am stupid, boring, unattractive, or inept, I will behave in a way that causes others to respond to me as if these things were true. It is in this way that we "act out" subjective truths so that they become objectively true. Subjective truths are self-confirming.

In the computer world there is a principle called GIGO—"garbage in, garbage out." Instruct a computer that two plus two equals five and it will operate on that principle. Thus a computer cannot perform any better than the information that is fed into it, no matter how sophisticated it is. At the level of subjective truths, we are much like the computers. If we have been programmed for a negative self-concept, our "output" in the form of behavior will be negative as well. We can be no better or happier than our own self-image.

Luckily, however, we have an advantage over the computers. We can learn to reprogram ourselves, rejecting or modifying the subjective truths that help determine our behavior. Many people are caught in a vicious cycle, where a negative and unhelpful self-concept produces negative experience that then serves to confirm the negative self-concept. But this vicious cycle can be broken.

Change is possible when you realize that the way you are does *not* come from objective permanent conditions. Your picture of yourself comes simply from very understandable reactions to experiences you've had. To change this picture, you have to open your mental file and insert new, carefully planned experiences that will gradually change your old, negative subjective truths. When you understand how you came to believe such things, you become much more open to changing them through new insight and experience.

Many patients in psychotherapy question the value of exploring "ancient history" as a way of dealing with their problems. I have found, however, that time spent in tracking down the nature of the unhelpful subjective truths held by an individual is often the most direct path to a change in his or her life situation.

You can change your shyness! No matter how extreme your loneliness, how great your social anxiety, how poor your opinion of yourself, the way to change is there. The first step in the process of change is to understand that your behavior is the "acting out" of certain notions you believe are true about yourself. When you see that these notions are really conclusions that you have drawn from your experience, then you can begin to reopen old files and to question the old conclusions.

For change to occur, however, new kinds of experiences must go into your file. This means that you will have to take the risk of doing some things differently from the way you are accustomed. You will have to dare to act as if your old notions about yourself are not true. Fortunately, the way to successful change and to increased contact with others is not uncharted. The exercises, skills, and techniques presented in this book are the product of scientific research, clinical observation, and lengthy experience of specialists in human behavior. They can help you change your life if you will let them.

# THREE

# Taking Stock of Your Shyness

LAST WEEK I had a problem with my car. No great mechanic, I called my local service station attendant.

"My car won't start," I said.

"Oh," he replied.

"Well, can you get it started?" I asked, feeling annoyed.

"That depends on whether you can tell me what's wrong with it."

"How would I know?" I snapped in exasperation. "You're the mechanic." (How many times have my clients said, "How should I know? You're the psychologist.")

"Well, has it behaved this way before?" he asked.

"No, it's almost a new car."

"Well, does the key turn all the way around?"

"Certainly," I replied. "Do you think I'm a total dummy?"

"Does the starter motor turn over?" he asked, politely ignoring my comment.

"Yes," I said, "it seems to be cranking normally."

"But the engine doesn't fire, right?"

"Well," I said, uncertain now, "it did, for a few seconds, and then it died. Then it started again, ran for a few seconds, and died again. I haven't been able to start it since."

"Right," said the mechanic. "I'll be over in ten minutes with a can of gas."

By insisting that I go beyond my original statement and give a careful description of exactly what happened, when it happened, and in what sequence it happened, my friend the mechanic was able to pinpoint the exact nature of my car's trouble and to solve it simply. If he had accepted my vague description of the problem, he might have wasted his time and my money by dispatching his fully equipped road service truck instead of bringing a gallon of gas.

Most folks who become aware that they have a problem in making contact with other people initially describe that problem in similarly vague terms. "I'm shy," they say, or "I don't get on well with people," or "I'm just not a social person." These descriptions are about as helpful as my statement, "My car won't start."

It's not hard to understand why we use such generalizations. They let us admit there's a problem without having to recall all the pain, shame, and anxiety of the problem itself. It *is* painful to remember episodes of failure. It *does* produce anxiety to recall the hundreds of little discomforts that, through their sheer repetition, trained us to be the way we are. It *is* embarrassing to hear again the voices from our past suggesting that we are not beautiful or interesting or smart. And it *is* distinctly uncomfortable to describe in graphic detail the whos, whats, whens, and wheres of our problem behavior.

Nevertheless, this kind of detailed description is what we need if we are to make any real attempt to deal with the problem of shyness. The task is to translate our general subjective truths (statements about what I am) into precise behavioral descriptions (statements about what I do, how I feel, and what happens in specific situations).

Why is this step so important? If you can translate general subjective truths into descriptions of what you do and how you feel in problem situations, you can change the focus of your problem entirely. We all believe that we are what we are—and there is no easy way to change a whole personality. But if the problem can be reduced to particular kinds of behavior—well, behavior is not so hard to change. It will take time, patience, and lots of practice, but it can be done. And once behavior begins to change, you can open the files on your negative ideas about yourself and begin to change them too.

The degree and extent of shyness vary a great deal among people. There are those whose every interaction with other people is painful and frustrating. They are close-mouthed and silent at home, withdrawn and unobtrusive at work, have few if any close friends, exhibit wallflower behavior at parties and other social occasions. Others are shy and uncomfortable only in specific situations—in fact, outside these situations they don't seem shy at all. Let's consider a few real cases to illustrate the degrees of shyness.

Viveca came to my office for help at age forty-seven, following a divorce from her husband of twenty-six years. Prior to her divorce, Viveca was not fully aware of how shy she was. Her husband, an aggressive, talkative, confident person, had provided an extensive camouflage for her. She had never worked, and had no friends except for a few couples she had met through her husband. He made all the family's major purchases, ordered for her when they ate out, and carried her end of the conversation as well as his own in social situations. Viveca's only meaningful method of expressing herself was in her paintings, which were powerful statements of deep thought and feeling.

Her divorce had laid bare the true extent of her problem. Living alone, she was reluctant to leave her apartment for any reason. She avoided making purchases of things she needed, from fear of dealing with sales people. Yet she had bought several quite unneeded items because she couldn't say no to salesmen who caught her attention. She felt terribly alone, yet because social situations aroused anxiety, she avoided places and activities that might bring her into contact with others. Most recently, she had begun to develop several illnesses that seemed to have no physical basis, but that always had the effect of preventing her from getting out of her self-constructed shell.

Tom was a talented, good-looking, thirty-one-year-old banking executive whose rise in position with his bank had been almost meteoric. In the less than four years since he had been employed by the bank as a management trainee, he had moved through several branch managerships to his current position as vice president in charge of market planning. He was married to an attractive, vivacious woman and was the father of two lovely children. Socially very active, he was a leader in his local Jaycee chapter, president of a mountaineers club, and on the board of a volunteer social service agency.

Tom sought therapy because of a problem of shyness in one particular situation. Now that he held a high managerial position at the bank, he attended executive conferences where the bank's overall policy was determined. These conferences were very informal and were attended only by the vice presidents and the president. Tom had been accustomed to delivering speeches and other public presentations of his work, but he discovered that when he was asked to give an off-the-cuff opinion at one of these executive meetings, he became tongue-tied and was gripped by a panic that was a total mystery to him. He became short of breath, his face flushed, and his voice trembled as he searched for weak excuses to explain his poor performance. When he came to me, he felt he must either solve this problem or suffer permanent damage to his career.

Leith was a nineteen-year-old university junior. Attractive and bubbly, she was a spark plug of dorm social events, and the life of every party she attended. Her activities as a cheerleader, a representative to the student senate, and a volunteer hospital worker put her in contact with hundreds of people each week, and she felt comfortable and at ease with all of them.

She sought treatment because of one gap in her pattern of social success. She reported that whenever she had a date, which was often, she utterly froze whenever she and her date were alone together.

Whenever there were other people present, she was her usual effervescent self, but alone in a car or when saying good night, Leith fell into an internal panic. She was unable to carry on a normal conversation, let alone be physically affectionate. Totally preoccupied with her inner confusion, she sometimes failed even to hear what her date was saying. Her behavior turned off most of her dates and promised to make it difficult for her to establish any lasting relationship with a man.

Terry was a salesman with a problem. He sold his plumbing business when he was thirty-six in the hope of making more money under more pleasant conditions by selling plumbing equipment to retail distributors. He was normally soft-spoken, an easygoing guy who had little difficulty relating to his wife, his children, and his friends. He found, however, that his contacts with potential clients, many of whom he had known for years, were characterized by a new kind of tension and stiffness. He would trudge through his sales presentation, unable to modify or deviate from his previously memorized pitch. Questions or comments from his customers seemed to throw him off the track, leaving him adrift and confused. Worse yet, when it came time to actually ask for a sale, he would often retreat, thanking the clients for their time, as if the only reason he had come was to show samples of his products. By the time Terry came for treatment, he had developed so much anxiety about these experiences that he was avoiding making his sales calls and was rapidly exhausting his savings to cover his fixed living expenses.

It is clear from these descriptions that Viveca, the housewife, had the most serious case of shyness. It extended to almost every area of her life and even made it difficult for her to cope with everyday decisions. This type of shyness I call _chronic._ I learned, as I talked further with Viveca, that the roots of her shyness went far back into childhood. Long before her marriage she had closed the file on a very negative and unhelpful self-image. She believed herself not worth being around, not worth listening to, not worth being considered in any way except to give other people (including her former husband and the salesmen who sold her unwanted items) the satisfactions they seemed to need. Through most of her marriage Viveca had never questioned these conclusions, but when her husband left her she was forced to reconsider her whole attitude toward herself and toward the world in general. We first explored her specific actions designed to keep others away and talked out the fears and anxiety she felt around other people. Overcoming shyness that is as severe and long-standing as Viveca's is a long, difficult process, but eventually Viveca, using many of the techniques suggested in this book, began to improve.

The situations of the three others—Tom, Leith, and Terry—were less difficult. The descriptions of their cases make it clear that for each, shyness was a problem only in a particular situation. Still, the problems of all three were serious and painful, threatening to limit their lives in important ways.

Tom had come from a very religious family with a powerful, strong-willed father. Every evening after dinner, the family would gather together for a devotional period. One of the activities during this time was a deadly serious "game" in which the father would randomly ask Tom or one of his two sisters to quote from the catechism or from the Bible. If they were successful, the children were rewarded with praise and increases in their weekly allowances. If not, there was disapproval and assigned study time for the learning of the Scriptures. Tom remembered these times as periods of extreme tension for him.

After fifteen years, these ordeals had come back to haunt Tom in the form of the executive conferences at the bank. The similarities between the two situations were very striking. Now Tom competed with other vice presidents instead of his sisters. His autocratic father had been replaced by the powerful bank president. Instead of Bible verses, he was being called on for off-the-cuff market analyses. Instead of praise and more allowance, he was performing for professional recognition and advancement. In the new situation he fell back into his old pattern of behavior and was unable to perform effectively.

Exploration of Leith's history showed that she also was responding to elements of an anxiety-arousing situation that had occurred years before. During her junior high years she regularly babysat for a couple who were good friends of her parents. Soon the man of the family, her "uncle," began to show his affection for her with secret caresses that were clearly sexual in nature, even to her uninitiated mind. Later he made more aggressive advances when he drove her home, and she had to wrestle him away. Finally she was able to discourage his attentions by threatening to tell her parents and his wife, but the situation had taught her to respond with deep anxiety to any situation in which she was alone with a man. By the time she was in college, the response was inappropriate, but it still reappeared whenever she was alone with a date, especially if they were in a car.

The origin of Terry's sales problem was more straightforward. He had learned to feel anxious and shy in a sales situation by being anxious and shy in a sales situation. During the summer immediately following his graduation from high school, he had taken a job as a door-to-door salesman of encyclopedias, a job that promised stupendous financial gain. He soon discovered that the sales pitch he was expected to use was not altogether honest and that many householders would not permit him even to get his foot in the door. Terry experienced polite no's, doors slammed in his face, and less-than-polite invitations to get lost. And when he did get to make his pitch he was ashamed and embarrassed. He finished the summer with a grand total of two sales, one of which was not completed because the customer failed to pass the company's credit investigation. Terry "forgot" the experience. But when he became a salesman again, he discovered that his anxiety response to selling encyclopedias had been generalized in his mind to cover all sales situations.

Now it's time for you to pinpoint the exact nature of your shyness. Are you like Viveca, shy in most situations where you find yourself in contact with other people? Or does shyness occur as an uncharacteristic reaction in an otherwise successful social life? My own area of shy-

ness, like that of Tom, Leith, and Terry, is situational—
I relate very poorly on the telephone. I suspect that I
learned this behavior because I depend on the nonverbal reactions of others to me and what I'm saying. Since
I'm used to watching the facial expressions of others to
see "how I'm doing," I feel lost on the telephone. In a
later chapter I'll tell what I did to get over this problem.

For you to take complete stock of your own kind of
shyness, the following pages present three simple exercises that will help you put the information in good
order. They are not "tests," being solely intended for
your own use. But devoting an hour or two to these
exercises will be very valuable to you in making use of
the information in the chapters that follow.

## *Self-Image Inventory*

Since shyness begins with one or a series of the subjective truths that you hold, a good way for you to begin
to focus on the specific nature of your shyness is to
catalog the content of these subjective truths. How
would you describe yourself to yourself? Spend fifteen
minutes on the following four questions, making lists of
as many words or phrases as you think describe yourself. You can be honest—no one need ever see these
answers except you.

When you have finished answering, go back over
your entire list and place a plus mark (+) in front of
things you like or feel are okay about yourself, and a
minus mark (−) in front of those things you don't like
or wish were different about yourself.

## SELF-IMAGE INVENTORY

1. *What do you look like?* (Include descriptions of such details as hair, teeth, eyes, weight, height, clothes; and such general considerations as sexual attractiveness, cleanliness, carriage, expression, etc.)

2. *How does your mind work?* (Quick, slow, thorough or not, well-informed or not, etc.)

3. *What do other people think you're like?*

4. *How well do you do on the job?* (Well, adequately, or poorly, enthusiastic or not, etc.)

The concentration of your minus marks will provide a clue as to whether your shyness is chronic or situational. If almost all your minus marks are under one of the four headings, you can be fairly sure your shyness is situational—confined to situations where that part of you comes into play. If, however, your minus marks are spread more or less evenly over the four areas, it's probable that your shyness is more general or chronic.

You can also get a rough idea of how severe your

shyness is by noting the proportion of minus marks to plus marks. If 25 percent or less of your answers are marked with minuses, chances are that your shyness is mild and shows up in only a few situations. If minus marks make up 25 to 50 percent of the total, you are moderately shy. If 50 to 75 percent of your answers are minuses, your shyness is fairly severe and will show up often and painfully. If more than 75 percent of your answers are minuses, your shyness is very severe and your feelings of inadequacy probably dominate almost all your relationships with others. Many people whose shyness is severe seek help from professional counselors.

To illustrate how the Self-Image Inventory works, here is Viveca's:

1. *What do you look like?*

      (−) dumpy                     (−) glasses
      (−) poor hair                 (−) cheap clothes
      (−) wrinkled neck             (+) nice teeth
      (−) flat-chested              (−) fat thighs
      (+) smooth, clear skin        (+) good use of make-
      (+) pretty nails                   up

2. *How does your mind work?*

      (−) dumb                      (+) ironically humorous
      (−) uneducated                (−) anxious
      (−) scatterbrained            (−) fearful
      (−) worrywart                 (−) sick
      (−) forgetful                 (+) interested in art

3. *What do other people think you're like?*

(−) shallow      (+) basically kind
(−) silly      (−) naive
(−) withdrawn      (−) sometimes don't
(−) strange         even notice me

4. *How are you at your work?*

(−) I don't have any!      (−) don't know what I
(−) untrained         could do
(+) paint okay      (−) don't feel well
(−) would be slow to         enough to work
     learn a job

Viveca is chronically and severely shy. The even spread of negative answers over all four areas tells us her shyness is not confined to any particular kind of situation, but rather pervades all her interactions with others. The high percentage of minus responses (78 percent) indicates her degree of shyness is rather extreme.

Tom's inventory, on the other hand, reveals a kind of shyness that is narrowly defined:

1. *What do you look like?*

(+) neat      (+) regular features
(+) well dressed      (+) good grooming
(+) good color and      (−) tendency to get
     texture of hair         skin blemishes
(+) in good shape

2. *How does your mind work?*

(+) analytic                    (−) sometimes not
(+) logical                        sensitive
(+) precise                     (−) not quick
(+) careful                     (−) tend to dwell on
(+) well educated                  things

3. *What do other people think you're like?*

(+) talented                    (+) an "up and comer"
(+) bright                      (+) good looking
(+) knowledgeable               (−) a little cold
(+) responsible                 (−) a bit stiff

4. *How are you at your work?*

(+) careful                        experience)
(+) thorough                    (+) competitive
(−) don't know as               (−) worried about how
    much as I should                co-workers see me
(−) not quick                   (−) afraid I'm going to
(−) think I may be                  make a big mistake
    too young for my            (−) poor at extempor-
    job (not enough                 aneous speaking

Tom's profile tells us that his self-image is mainly
positive since 64 percent of his answers are positive. In
the first three categories his positive answers are 73
percent of the total. But in the fourth category negative
answers outnumber the positive. It's no surprise that
Tom's shyness should emerge in severe form at work.
Analyzing your own Self-Image Inventory in a simi-

lar way, you should learn more about your subjective truths. The results may surprise you at first, but if you've been honest, they will tell you some important things about yourself.

## *Behavioral Shyness Inventory*

The next step is to translate your general impression of yourself into behavioral descriptions. As we've already discussed, this translation is essential to overcoming your problem—whether it is mild or severe. From here on, we're not interested in what you think about yourself; we're interested in *what you do* and *how you feel* in certain situations. The first step is to answer the questions below.

BEHAVIORAL SHYNESS INVENTORY
Answer each question "True" (T) or "False" (F).

___F___ 1. I notice that my hands sometimes sweat as I talk to other people.

___F___ 2. I seldom begin a conversation. Usually I wait to see what someone else is going to say.

___T___ 3. I worry often about whether I look okay.

___F___ 4. Parties are usually uncomfortable for me.

___F___ 5. I sometimes have trouble controlling my voice when I'm talking to a group of people.

___F___ 6. Times when I've had to make a speech in public have been really upsetting to me.

_F_ 7. I can seldom think of anything intelligent to say.

_T_ 8. I wouldn't usually send an overdone steak back to the kitchen in a restaurant.

_F_ 9. I really get flustered when I feel a conversation is going badly.

_F_ 10. I have feelings I'd like to tell my mate about, but I almost never do.

_F_ 11. I get uncomfortable when people are looking at me.

_T_ 12. I get uncomfortable looking into someone's eyes for too long.

_T_ 13. Sometimes I get short of breath when I haven't been exerting myself.

_F_ 14. I've never asked for a raise or a promotion.

_F_ 15. Several times I've gotten unexplainably sick before a social occasion.

_F_ 16. I don't like to express opinions because I always feel I can't back them up.

_F_ 17. I usually sit or stand away from the middle of things in a group.

_F_ 18. I feel that I'm poorer with words than most people.

_F_ 19. I get panicky when I'm asked a question in a group of people.

_F_ 20. My panic is so intense it sometimes stops me from speaking altogether.

_T_ 21. I get butterflies in my stomach quite often.

_F_ 22. I don't like to talk with co-workers about

work because I feel they're better at it than
I.

_T_ 23. When I feel a contact with someone has
gone badly, I feel uncomfortable seeing him
again.

_F_ 24. Dating situations are tense and uncomfortable for me.

_T_ 25. Sometimes, in a social situation, some part
of my body begins to tremble uncontrolla-
bly.

_F_ 26. On a date I find myself at times worried
about my breath or the odor of my body.

_F_ 27. Initiating a social contact, particularly a
date, with someone else is almost impossible for me.

_F_ 28. There are often long, uncomfortable periods of silence when I can't think of what to
say.

These questions were designed to determine what
kind of shyness reactions you have—both physical and
mental—what outward shyness behavior you have, and
what kind of situations they appear in. This inventory
isn't a scientific instrument to measure your shyness or
to compare you with other shy people. It's simply a tool
for evaluating yourself and understanding your own
reactions.

## Shyness Chart

On the following Shyness Chart you can enter the results of the two exercises you have just completed. The chart can be filled out in the book or copied on another sheet of paper to allow more room. If you follow the directions, you will have a full summary of your shyness problem. The summary makes a perfect starting place for your campaign to overcome your problem and to begin making more satisfying contact with other people.

These are the directions for the Shyness Chart:

*Column 1.* In this column enter each of the descriptive words or phrases you marked with a minus on the Self-Image Inventory (page 39). These are some of the negative labels you have applied to yourself.

*Column 2.* Physical reactions accompanying shyness include blushing, trembling, muscle-tightening, etc. You show some of these signs if you marked any of the following questions "True" in the Behavioral Shyness Inventory (pages 43–45): 1, 5, 13, 15, 20, 21, and 25. For each of these questions marked "True," enter a key word or phrase in Column 2 of the chart.

*Column 3.* Mental reactions accompanying shyness include excessive concern with other people's evaluations of you, constant self-evaluation, and worries about the catastrophic outcome of a social contact. You show some of these signs if you answered "True" to questions 3, 7, 9, 11, 18, 23, and 26 in the Behavioral Shyness Inventory. For each "True" answer, enter a key word or phrase in Column 3.

*Column 4.* Shy behavior is usually easier to spot in others than in ourselves. Some of the signs are giving

MY SHYNESS CHART

| 1 | 2 | 3 | 4 | 5 |
|---|---|---|---|---|
| Because I have felt that I am | I experience physical reactions such as | and I think thoughts such as | and I end up looking like | in situations such as |

one-word answers to questions; avoiding expression of strong opinions or of feelings, wants, or preferences; not meeting others' eyes, etc. If you marked any of the following questions "True" in the Behavioral Shyness Inventory, you practice a shy behavior yourself: 2, 8, 12, 16, 17, 22, and 28. For each "True" answer, enter a key word or phrase in Column 4.

*Column 5.* As we have seen, different people suffer from shyness in different situations: some at work, some at parties and other social gatherings, some when alone with a member of the opposite sex. The questions 4, 6, 10, 14, 19, 21, 24, and 27 you marked "True" in the Behavioral Shyness Inventory will suggest where your shyness is most likely to surface. For each "True" answer, enter a key word or phrase in Column 5.

To understand how the Shyness Chart summarizes the elements of your shyness, look at the result of Tom's exploration of himself on the facing page.

Now that you have spent the time and energy to think about how you learned to be shy, and to discover the exact combination of physical, mental, behavioral, and situational factors that make up your unique brand of shyness, you have already moved a long way down the road to overcoming it. Once you begin to penetrate the emotional fog that has hidden your problem, you can see there are definite causes for your shyness and that it is not some mystical quality you were born with.

What remains is for you to learn, by a combined process of insight and practice, to apply new skills to the problem areas you have identified. As you do so, you will be "reopening the file" on your self-image, adding new experiences to the file, and re-forming your ideas about yourself in relationship to other people.

## MY SHYNESS CHART

| 1 | 2 | 3 | 4 | 5 |
|---|---|---|---|---|
| **Because I have felt that I am** | **I experience physical reactions such as** | **and I think thoughts such as** | **and I end up looking like** | **in situations such as** |
| blemishes | sweaty hands | can't think what to say | don't volunteer | public speaking |
| insensitive | trembly voice | upset when it starts to go bad | no eye contact | when asked a direct question |
| not quick | short of breath | don't like all of them looking at me | can't back opinion | talking with other V.P.'s |
| dwell on things | butterflies | poor use of words | sit on edge of group | |
| cold, stiff | knees tremble | afraid I'll make a mistake | don't talk with other V.P.'s | |
| worried about co-workers | | too young | | |

# FOUR

# How to Change the Way You Talk to Yourself

DOG TRAINERS KNOW that if a newborn Great Dane puppy is raised behind a two-foot fence, it will soon learn that the fence is an impassable barrier. At first, the dog will show interest in the fence, perhaps stand up against it, try to dig under it. But if he is unsuccessful in escaping, he soon quits trying altogether. The fence comes to mark the boundaries of the dog's life and "keeps him in his place."

The same dog a year later, 150 pounds heavier and thirty inches taller, could almost step over the two-foot fence, but to him it is still an impassable barrier. His early experiences caused him to conclude that the fence could not be crossed, and he "closed the file" on the subject. From then on, unless he is somehow retrained, he is confined—not by the fence, but by the idea that he holds about the fence.

We are not so different from the Great Dane. Our own negative conclusions, drawn from early experiences, can serve as barriers to our enjoyment of life and other people. Long after we forget the particular experiences that formed our conclusions, the conclusions themselves remain active and unchallenged in our minds.

I have said that these ideas are active. They aren't like stacks of merchandise in a warehouse. Our minds recreate our subjective truths from moment to moment—so that it is fair to say the truths are active and "alive." Even when we're not conscious of it, the mind goes on talking, repeating the ideas that are basic to our concept of ourselves, other people, and the world. Frederick Perls, a leader in the gestalt school of psychology, called this activity our "internal monologue." This monologue recreates, repeats, and reaffirms the ideas on which we base our lives. Whether we are awake or asleep, occupied or idle, our subconscious thoughts hammer away, reciting the guidelines of our existence.

The first step toward overcoming a problem such as shyness is to change the way you "talk to yourself." Your mind is constantly chanting, "I'm ugly, I'm dumb, I'm incompetent, I'm no good, I'm shy," and holding you back, causing fear and anxiety. But there are ways to change that internal singsong.

The first thing you'll need is a good imagination. Shy people are strange. On one hand, their imagination is overdeveloped; they can imagine the most exquisite social and personal disasters and are always fearing the worst. But about themselves, shy people have an underdeveloped imagination—they can't imagine that they themselves could ever be any different than they are. More than once, when I have suggested to a client a new kind of behavior in a social situation, the answer has been, "But that just isn't done!" What the client usually means is, "Why, *I* could never do that!"

I hasten to add that my suggestions in these cases were legal, moral, and usually very conventional. But to a shy client they seemed way out. I kept saying, "Don't rule it out . . . there's nothing wrong with it . . . imagine yourself as a new person." Now I say a similar thing to you. Cultivate the power of your imagination, because it will help invent the new ideas you'll need to overcome your shy behavior.

Actors and actresses use their imaginations temporarily to change their manner of talking to themselves and to change their behavior when they are preparing to perform a role in a play or movie. They consciously struggle to identify with a new set of thoughts, feelings, and behaviors that are not characteristic of them but that they intend to make their own, at least for the time of the performance. Often they need time after a performance to "come back to themselves." When you use your imagination you'll be doing much the same thing as the actor or actress, except that your goal will be permanent change.

All of your work so far has been analytical. You've uncovered some of the negative ideas in your concept of yourself. You've named much of the behavior these concepts produce, and you've identified some particular situations most likely to bring on a full-fledged attack of shyness. Now you are about to go a step further. In the future, how would you like to feel about yourself? How would you like to behave, even in the real "trouble" situations? What's your fantasy? Imagining a new you—creating your own new self-model—is the next crucial step on the road to making contact with others.

Follow these directions carefully.

*Step 1.* Sit down with your Shyness Chart from Chapter 3 (page 47). On a fresh piece of paper, copy down the words or phrases that are purely negative but not physically descriptive (such as "stupid" or "incompetent"); the phrases that begin with a physical description (such as "big, ugly nose") will be used in Step 2.

Beside each purely negative phrase write a *realistic positive comment* about yourself. Your attitudes in the past have been unrealistically negative. Don't go off to the other extreme, changing "stupid" to "most brilliant intellect since Socrates." Instead, think about the qualities that you like about yourself and that deserve development. If you're not brilliant, are you practical, do you have common sense, are you good with figures or machines or handicrafts? Don't let that old negative voice kill your enthusiasm now—use your imagination!

*Step 2.* Now write down every statement from the Shyness Chart that is a negative evaluation of a physical characteristic. Next to each of these statements write the same thing in a purely descriptive manner. For example, change "flat-chested" to "size 34-A brassiere." Don't be afraid to be a bit humorous if you're inclined. Humor can put things in their proper perspective. For example, instead of "big, ugly nose," you might write something like, "My nose associates me with such famous men as W. C. Fields, Cyrano de Bergerac, Danny Thomas, and Jimmy Durante." However you do it, rewrite the original statement, keeping the description but eliminating the negative evaluation.

*Step 3.* Go back to your Self-Image Inventory (page 39) and write down each of the items you marked with a plus.

*Step 4.* Now you have modified some of your negative ideas of yourself (Step 1), eliminated your negative evaluations of physical characteristics (Step 2), and collected your positive ideas about yourself (Step 3). The next step is to put all these things together into a new "Self-Description."

The Self-Description will point a new direction for you—the direction you want to go in the coming weeks and months. It should not ignore the facts. For example, if you are five feet tall, your new self-description can't advertise you as being 6-foot-6. But beginning with your positive feelings about yourself, the Self-Description should describe you as you hope to be three months or six months from now, describing new and more positive attitudes and behavior.

If you're comfortable with pencil and paper, sit down and write a short essay, using the statements you have developed in Steps 1, 2, and 3. If writing is difficult for you, try dictating your Self-Description into a cassette tape recorder, speaking slowly and pausing after each sentence. Whichever method you use, you'll probably have to make several drafts before you're satisfied. Give yourself several days, beginning when you're relaxed and rested and stopping when you begin to feel tired or frustrated.

Use your imagination, and try to picture yourself acting in new ways in familiar anxiety situations. Don't fall back on generalities, using such words as "poise," "confidence," and the like. Instead, picture in your mind how you will look and act, what you will say and how you will feel as your new self. Be specific and detailed and work toward making striking pictures of your new behavior both in your own mind and in your written or recorded Self-Description.

Here is what Viveca's Self-Description might have looked like. (If you want to recall Viveca's story, look back at pages 31–32. Her Self-Image Inventory is on pages 40–41.)

> My name is Viveca G. I am 5-foot-5, and weigh 145 pounds. I would like to weigh 125, and have plans to make that happen. I have strawberry blonde hair that is somewhat thin, but nicely styled and cared for. Physically, I am beginning to look like a mature woman of 45 (which I am), with small wrinkles appearing at my neck. I wear a size 36-B brassiere. Two of my loveliest features are my smooth, clear skin and my strong, well-shaped nails, both of which I care for carefully.
>
> Although I did not go to college or trade school (and I often wish I had, and maybe I will yet!), I seem to be about as bright as most people I know. There are still many areas of knowledge, particularly in art, that I want to explore further. I am learning to organize my thoughts and my time more efficiently, and to relax in order to be free from worrying about things beyond my control. I have a nice, dry wit that I am finding people appreciate as I express it more each day. In the past I have had many fears that have even made me physically sick, but I grow stronger as I become more and more the good, strong, healthy person I know myself to be.
>
> I like people a great deal and enjoy being kind to them. I like the fact that I am not a "heavy," that is, I am not given to profound or particularly intense

comments. Sometimes I even like to be silly for a
while, going back for a few moments to a simple
humor of childhood. I often tend to be rather quiet,
but I am learning to be much more open, honest, and
trusting of other people as the days go by.

One of the major areas of adventure in my life
right now is in the world of work. Since my divorce
last year, I have been questioning what kind of work
will be best for me, both in terms of personal fulfill-
ment and financial gain. While I am aware I'm not
highly trained in any particular skill, I also know that
many occupations are open to me. The further I get
from my old tendency to downgrade myself and my
abilities, the more excited I become about support-
ing myself in a way that is fulfilling to me.

Notice how specific this self-description is. It responds to every element of Viveca's Self-Image Inventory. This mini-essay could be shortened to read, "I am
attractive, intelligent, confident with people, and looking forward to working." But such a summary would
overlook Viveca's specific situation and wouldn't help
her much in changing her attitudes and behavior. Remember that the part of your mind that processes subjective truths responds to concrete details and striking
pictures, not to broad generalities. Go back over your
own Self-Description sentence by sentence and ask,
"Can I be more specific?"

*Step 5.* Look back at your Shyness Chart (page 47).
Go over each of the problem situations listed in Column 5 of the chart. Then list them on a clean sheet of
paper, down the left margin, with the situation that
is *least* difficult for you at the top, and in order of

increasing difficulty. Set the sheet aside until Step 7.

*Step 6.* Now look at the entries in Columns 2, 3, and 4 of the Shyness Chart. These columns record your physical and mental reactions in problem situations and your typical shyness behaviors. List them at the left margin of a clean sheet of paper. Then write a clear sentence describing yourself reacting or behaving in exactly *the opposite* way. Again, be specific and work at imagining your new feelings and actions.

*Step 7.* Return to the sheet you made in Step 5. Opposite each of your problem situations, write a short paragraph beginning, "Whenever I [am in this situation] . . ." Then complete the paragraph by using appropriate sentences from Step 6. When the paragraphs are complete, add them to your Self-Description essay.

Here is the way Tom might have done Step 7 (see pages 32–33, 35–36, 41–42 and 49 for material about Tom):

> When I am in conference with our banking group, I really feel as if I belong. Though I am young, this fact only points more to my ability in the field. Sitting among my co-workers, I feel calm, relaxed, and part of a team working for the same goals. Because my attention is focused on the issues at hand, and not on myself, I am not aware of any physical feeling other than calm, relaxed concentration.
>
> When I am called upon with advance notice to present some material from my department to the group, I prepare it carefully, and I come to the meeting feeling very sure that I know my material well. As I speak, my voice is clear, firm, and distinct. My breathing is deep and regular. My body feels quite

relaxed. When I look up from my notes, I look at my listeners, taking care to make eye contact with several of them.

When I am spontaneously asked a direct question in the group meetings, I am usually aware of the answer, because I have been following the discussion. I feel calm and relaxed. I have no worries about giving the "right" answer because, after all, I am the expert in that area. That's why I am asked the question! When I honestly do not know the answer, I feel comfortable in smiling, meeting the questioner's eyes, and saying, "I don't know, but it's a good question and I'll find out for you." I know and understand clearly that this situation is not like the old Bible test situations my Dad used to conduct. I have already been rewarded by the very fact that I am in the group, and I will not be punished for not giving the "right answer."

*Step 8.* Your Self-Description now contains two parts: The first is your own new self-image, and the second is your desired new behavior in problem situations. When it is as clear and specific as you can make it, either rewrite it very clearly on a new sheet of paper or record it on a cassette tape recorder, speaking very clearly and distinctly and pausing for fifteen seconds after each sentence. The Self-Description is a basic piece of study material for you. From here on, your job will be to get its message to sink into your mind.

*Step 9.* Pick a time of day when you will have an opportunity to relax completely and let your imagination work with the material you have assembled in the Self-Description. In my experience, the times just before bed (if you can stay awake) or first thing in the

morning are most beneficial. A midday break can also
be good, if you can allow enough time.

Strange as it seems, you may have to practice a few
separate exercises just to learn to relax. If you find it a
problem to unwind enough to concentrate, see the
sample relaxation exercises in the Appendix.

Find a quiet place, free from distractions. Get as comfortable as you can, lying down if possible. Spend the
first ten minutes unwinding and relaxing—by using
your own method or one of the exercises in the Appendix. Then put on the Self-Description tape or read
aloud your Self-Description, one sentence at a time,
pausing for fifteen seconds after each sentence. During
the pauses, try to picture as vividly as you can what you
have just heard or read. Don't be discouraged if at first
you have trouble picturing the images. After all, you've
had a great deal of practice at *not* using your imagination in this way. You'll be amazed at how rapidly you
learn to picture the images you present to yourself.
Soon you'll be able to wind out whole one-act plays in
your mind in which you will finally be the hero, not the
goat.

The important thing about this exercise is that it be
repeated *without fail* every day. Your internal monologue has been repeating negative things for years and
years. You will have to listen to your "new" voice quite
a few times and you must learn to relax and really hear
what the new voice is saying. Make this learning session
a part of your daily routine and give it a chance to work.

*Step 10.* After two weeks of practicing at least once
a day, reserve a normal practice period to contemplate
changes that have occurred in you. There will be some,

although they may not be obvious at first. Generally, you notice that you are a little more relaxed in what used to be your "panic" situations. Oh yes, and there was the time you volunteered a comment when you were with a group. Remember the time you were introduced to that friend of your friend and you noticed you acted a bit less shy? These small individual advances will promote a kind of snowball effect, so that your personal growth away from shyness will gain momentum as time passes.

## Finding a Role Model

Psychologist Albert Bandura has discovered that a person can often learn new behavior by imitating the actions of another person. He called this method of learning "modeling" because the learners seemed to imitate a "model" whose actions brought the desired results or rewards.

Even our Great Dane puppy could demonstrate this technique of learning. If another Great Dane, who is not "bound in" by the idea of the two-foot fence, comes into the pen, it will effortlessly jump over the fence. Our growing pup watches and cocks his head in wonder at the feat. After watching the performance two or three times, he goes over and sniffs the fence as if to assure himself that the fence is still there. Tentatively he puts a paw over, then his head, and before you know it he is standing on the other side, wondering how he got there. Within a short time he is jumping the fence whenever he wants, scarcely remembering his earlier misconception.

Human experience is also full of examples of modeling. Athletes study films of the greats in order to model their golf swing, boxing stance, or pattern of broken-field running. Actors and actresses frequently study the movements, facial expressions, and deliveries of great actors in order to develop their own styles. Deaf children are taught to speak by imitating the mouth movements of their teacher.

You can also employ the principle of modeling to learn how to be a "contactful" person. This method is a good back-up to the ten-step method just described. Modeling has the advantage of providing a live demonstration of the behavior you want to learn and gives you the assurance that the new behavior "works."

First you must identify the problem situations in which you would like to change your reactions and behavior. You can do this by following Steps 1 through 7 above. Then think of someone you know who handles such situations in a way you admire. The person does not have to be someone you admire wholeheartedly or would like to be (after all, the person you really want to be is yourself). But you should know that he or she can produce effectively the behaviors you would like to produce. Put yourself in a position to watch that person in the appropriate situation. Note everything he or she does, down to the smallest detail. Later, in private, list these observations one by one on a sheet of paper. It may take you several watching sessions to get down all the details.

Now write a mini-essay describing the successful behavior as you observed it, but write it as if *you* were the one in that rewarding role. The final result will look much like the material you wrote in Step 7 above.

When your description of the new behavior is as detailed and specific as you can make it, follow Steps 8 through 10 above. After two weeks of imagination practice, try out the new behavior in real life. Don't try to make it happen all at once. Instead, make it your first goal to act out the first sentence of your description. Then try the next sentence, and so on. In a remarkably short time you will find yourself sailing over that particular "shyness fence" as though it had never existed.

I mentioned earlier that I have had a particular shyness problem with telephone conversations. When I decided to do something about it, I used the modeling method. This is how I did it:

First, I noted that when I made a call, I had some mild physical reactions of anxiety—butterflies, and a clipped, tense tone in my voice. Then I noted some problem thoughts, like, "I'm afraid I'll be interrupting something" and "I'm afraid he or she won't know who I am." And then I spotted some problem behaviors—I spoke too softly and too fast, and I plunged right into my business without any preliminaries. For each problem behavior, I wrote a sentence indicating how I would like to be.

I didn't have to look far for a role model. The person who best fit my description of how I would like to be on the phone was then my roommate, Frank. I knew, both from having spoken to him on the phone and from hearing him talk to others, that he was warm, easy, relaxed, and yet highly efficient in telephone conversation.

I began to observe Frank as he talked to people over

the phone from our living room. I observed the following things:

1. He got himself comfortable on the couch or easy
   chair before dialing. He almost never made a call
   standing up.
2. When his call was answered, he smiled and said,
   "Hi, _____, this is Frank."
3. He always asked, "Have you got a few minutes to
   talk?"
4. He asked a question about how the person he was
   calling was doing, including in his question a personal detail he knew about in that person's life.
5. He would tell about some experience he had recently had that was not related to the business of
   his call.
6. When he had completed all of the above, he
   would state the purpose of his call clearly and
   directly.
7. If some decision had been reached during the
   conversation, he would restate it before ending,
   and ask if his restatement was correct ("Okay,
   we're meeting at your place at seven on Thurs-
   day evening, is that right?").
8. He always ended with a comment of appreciation like, "It's been good to talk to you."

When I felt I understood exactly what Frank was
doing over the phone, I wrote my mini-essay in which
I was performing exactly the same routine. After a few
sessions of imaginative practice (it did not take even
close to two weeks, because it was such a narrowly
defined problem), I felt I was ready to put the new

behavior into practice. Because the problem was one of telephoning, I was able to make a list of the things I wanted to do and to check them off one by one as I did each in my phone conversation. Almost before I knew it, my phone conversations were better, I was feeling better about myself, and I had opened up a new way to do business, conduct personal relationships, and remain in contact with more people more often.

Learning to change the way you talk to yourself will take some time and lots of effort. Especially important are three points that we have already mentioned, but which bear repeating.

First, in your Self-Description and in your practice sessions, think as concretely and specifically as you can. Make vivid mental pictures for yourself, not vague abstractions.

Second, take time to learn how to relax. Relaxation is a skill that usually is not given much value in our culture. But it's actually a secret tool that you can use to change and grow in the directions you want.

Third, and most important, be diligent in your daily repetitions of these methods. They would not be methods but miracles if they worked overnight. You have lived years, perhaps a lifetime, with shyness. Have the patience and the commitment to take a few weeks or months to learn how to overcome shyness and make contact with others. It will be worth it.

# FIVE

# How to Know What to Say— By Listening

WE HAVE ALREADY BEGUN to work on the feelings and attitudes that cause shy people to pull back from contact with others. We have uncovered common negative thoughts and have suggested ways in which you can change the way you talk to yourself. By the time you read this, I hope you have written your new Self-Description and set aside some time each day to work on your own attitudes.

It's time to move on, however, and begin to think about other people. How can you change the way you talk to them? Or, perhaps more to the point, how can you get over the urge *not* to talk to them, the urge to avoid contact?

Each individual shy person has his or her unique brand of shyness, but there are some common symptoms. For example, most shy people never initiate a conversation. They seldom look other people in the eye, and they avoid ever moving too close to them. They dress as unobtrusively as possible and take great care never to say or do anything that could attract unwelcome attention. If you behave in this fashion, you are an expert at avoiding contact with others.

## Thinking of Others

The first step toward breaking down this avoidance behavior is to examine the ways you feel different from other people. Of course, in many factual ways each of us *is* different. But at a deeper level, we are all very much the same. We all need the same things for survival, and experience the same emotions—love, hate, anger, joy, sorrow, sexual desire, and many others. And we all want the same things from others—love, acceptance, respect, a sense of importance, of belonging someplace, and of belonging with someone.

Dr. Carl Rogers, one of the most distinguished writers and thinkers about human relationships, has noted this fact and has summarized the basic underlying similarity among people in the statement, "What is most personal is most general." By this I understand him to mean that when I tell you the relatively impersonal facts about myself, those facts distinguish me from you. But when I tell you the very personal things about myself, such as how lonely I feel in a strange city, or how I felt when my marriage ended, or what I hope for from my life, they turn out to be the things you yourself have experienced and can share, and that brings us closer together.

When I point out this essential similarity of people to a shy person, he or she will often smile knowingly and say, "Yes, but I'm shy and you're not"—as if this were evidence of some essential difference between us. If this means that the person worries about how other people will respond to him or her and is afraid of being disliked or rejected, why, that is no difference at all. I and everyone else I have ever known experience the same worries. The shy person's fears may be more intense and may lead to behavior that cuts off contact with others, but the fears themselves are *human* fears and are shared by everyone.

Think this through for a moment. If you are shy, the difference between you and nonshy people is not that you have fears and worries and they don't. The difference is in how you cope with your fears. Nonshy people find ways to make contact with others in spite of their worries, but you have acquired mannerisms that warn others to stay away from you. Your shyness has become a self-constructed prison: Out of fear of being found different or inferior, you have developed patterns of behavior that deprive you of your rightful share of love, acceptance, recognition, and respect.

One of the keys to breaking out of this prison is to think long and hard about the other people you know. Has it occurred to you that they are really seeking the same things you are? In a way, this observation is obvious. But many shy people are so self-involved, listening only to the small, scared voices inside themselves, that they don't really consider other people's needs and desires.

To be fair, this failure to consider others is not confined to shy people. Our society places a peculiar emphasis on competing to achieve recognition from others. Can I be so attractive, so winning, so witty, that you have no choice but to love me? Can I demonstrate that I am so bright, so powerful, so commanding that you will have to respect me? Can I be so charming, so quick, so profound, so funny, or perhaps even so loud that you must pay attention to me? Such aggressive behavior is likely to be no more satisfying than the shy person's withdrawal.

Between the social isolation of shyness and the superficial contact of aggressiveness, there is a middle course that leads to genuine contact. And the first step along this road is to acknowledge that other people, in ways that are truly important, are very like ourselves and that their needs are as important to them as ours are to us. The people who are successful in making contact with others have learned to give what they themselves would like to receive. They give love to those by whom they would be loved. They respect those by whom they would be respected. They show their liking for people they want to like them.

This key principle helps explain why you, as a shy person, have not been regularly close to anyone in the past. Your behavior has been principally self-centered. When you have been around other people, your concerns have focused on yourself. You worry about whether you look all right, and miss entirely how the other person looks to you. You waste your energy and attention judging yourself, and have none left over to be aware of the other. So much of your attention has been caught up with your own anxiety that you miss whatever the other person may be caught up with or may be feeling. You receive little from others, then, not because you are fat, not because you are ugly, not because you are dumb, but simply because you *give* so little.

## Active Listening

How can you begin to give others these elusive but highly valuable gifts of love, respect, and recognition? We made one kind of beginning in the last chapter, and your new way of talking to yourself should help you to see yourself and others in a new light. But now you are ready to make new contacts—particularly to begin talking to others.

The most frequently stated complaint of shy people is, "I never know what to say." Shy people frequently get caught in situations where they appear to be completely tongue-tied, unable to come up with even a semblance of a response. Behind the blank stare and the silence rages a storm of emotional upheaval, with boiling clouds of anxiety, lightning bolts of fear, and an occasional thunderclap of outright panic.

We've already discussed ways to calm that storm. Now I'll suggest another. Forget your worry about what to say and *listen* to what the other person is saying. The way to making conversation is through the ears.

If you're like many of the shy folks I've talked with in my office, your first reaction to the notion of becoming a good listener is, "My God, how can you say such a thing? Here I've been sitting for ninety percent of my life with my mouth shut and you have the nerve to tell me that learning to listen is a part of overcoming shyness!"

Well, it is. Keeping your mouth shut and listening are two entirely different activities. It's true that you've been listening for a good part of your life, but what you've been listening to has been your own anxiety, the ceaseless chanting of self-deprecating slogans in your own head. Shy people don't listen to other people, they listen to all those worried little voices inside themselves.

Don't think that shy people have a monopoly on non-listening. What usually passes for conversation in our society is really an activity in which a person politely waits for others to finish talking about themselves so that he can have a turn talking about himself. Simon and Garfunkel described this kind of talk as "The Sound of Silence."

Think for a minute of someone who might serve as a model for making conversation. At one time or another, you have probably met someone who has broken through your shyness, at least for the moment, and made you feel happy and important. If you think back carefully, you'll discover that that person listened to every word you had to say, no matter how trivial it seemed, never expecting you to be earthshaking or witty. He or she seemed to enjoy what you had to say and showed a desire to understand you better by asking pertinent questions and encouraging you to go on.

That person was a skillful listener. If you recall the experience, you'll realize that it was intensely pleasurable. It was a real boost to find that your thoughts and feelings and experiences were interesting enough to somebody else that he or she gave the time and energy to really listen and understand. It was a relief not to have to compete with that person to get your two cents in; you had all the time you needed to express yourself fully. You even found that when someone else was really listening, you were able to hear yourself a little better.

A conversation like this also leaves you with good feelings toward the other person. He created a space in which both of you belonged comfortably, and he showed no sign of judging or criticizing you. You began to feel that it was safe and secure to be yourself, and you soon concluded that you would like to speak with him again—soon. As these experiences mount up, you find the other person has become an important source of pleasure in your life.

People are not born skillful listeners any more than people are born shy. Skillful listening is a fairly complex activity, but we can break it down into individual actions, study the actions, and learn to repeat them. With practice you can learn to be a skillful listener too.

Dr. Carl Rogers, whom we mentioned earlier, began some thirty years ago to develop a type of psychotherapy based on good listening. One person (the therapist) helps another (the client) solely by attempting to hear and fully understand what the client has to say. Rogers called this form of therapy "client-centered therapy" because it depends on what is said by the client, rather than by the therapist. The client is free to find himself and be himself without any fear that the therapist will dispute, ridicule, or try to correct any of his statements. The therapist's only role is to try to understand what the client is saying so fully that he actually begins to understand what it feels like to be that person.

The therapist in this type of therapy must make it clear to the client that he or she is being understood—not judged or analyzed. In order to accomplish this, Rogers developed a way of talking that is really just listening. He called this way of talking "reflexive listening." Other psychologists have come to call it "active listening."

All this talk of psychotherapy is important to your problem of shyness because the technique of active listening can be removed from the counseling office and used by anyone who wants to make contact with another human being.

Here are six easy rules that, if you learn to follow them, will make you a good active listener:

1. Listen carefully to what the other person is saying.
2. In your response, try to rephrase or restate the exact meaning of what has just been said.
3. Don't add any opinions, thoughts, or feelings of your own unless the other person asks for them.
4. Never ridicule or be sarcastic about someone else's comments.
5. Respond with questions beginning, "Do you mean . . ." "Are you saying . . ." or "Is this what I hear you saying . . ."
6. If a pause occurs in the conversation, ask a question of your own.

Active listening gives other persons the important gifts of respect, attention, and recognition, and leaves them with warm feelings toward the listener. A striking side benefit for you, the listener, is that you can say good-bye forever to that old fear that you won't be able to think of something to say. The person you're talking to is telling you what to say every time he or she speaks!

## Starting a Conversation

There's only one flaw in active listening, you may say. You can see how it works, but in a normal social situation, how can you get a conversation started? Before you can listen to someone, you must get him talking to you.

Most shy people are in the habit of keeping others from talking to them and have learned to be terribly afraid of what will happen if someone does. What the shy person does not recognize is that most people have the same ambivalent feelings about beginning a conversation. Almost everyone feels some pangs of anxiety during the first few moments. Will I say the right thing? Will the other person think I'm okay?

How do nonshy people ever get a conversation started, then? Well, consciously or not, they have learned a very simple, straightforward technique for beginning a conversation: asking a *ritual question.*

As a group, shy people are reluctant to ask any questions at all. The reason they give is that they don't want to intrude on someone else's privacy. I suspect that the real reason is the old fear of being thought stupid. If I ask a question, I'm proclaiming to the world that I don't know the answer, and if I don't know the answer, then I must be stupid! No one, of course, could carry off such horrible reasoning if they were not convinced of their own inferiority in the first place.

Nonshy people use ritual questions as a way of "breaking the ice" at the beginning of a conversation. Some common examples of ritual questions are "Where are you from?" "What do you do?" and even "What's your name?" These questions are called ritual questions because, although they are phrased like standard questions (requests for information), their primary purpose is really to convey a message. The message is, "I am interested in you" and "I think I would like to know you."

Many shy folks I've known experience a fear that a ritual question from them will offend the person they want to approach. Indeed, you can probably expect to feel a bit scared the first few times you try it. After all, you have spent a great deal of time developing and maintaining your anxiety in social encounters. It would be very strange if that response magically disappeared. Remember, however, that all people are flattered and gratified by attention and interest. Rather than feeling that you are invading their privacy, the persons you address are more likely to feel "How nice that you too feel I'm important." Contrary to your fear that they will think your question is stupid, their subconscious reaction will probably be, "How intelligent you are to be curious about me."

Here is a list of ritual questions that you can use to begin a conversation:

"Hi! My name is _____. What's yours?"

"Where are you from? Are you enjoying the area?"

"What do you do? What do you like to do when you're not working? Have you been in the business a long time?"

"How are you enjoying the [party, convention, class, flight, etc.]?"

"Your ring looks Indian—is it?"

"What year are you in school? What do you want
to do when you graduate?"
"What's your major?"

Even when you are using the very powerful combination of ritual questions and active listening, pauses or
lapses in conversation will sometimes happen. If you
are just learning to make contact through conversation,
you may begin to panic at this point because you feel
it is your turn to think of some bright, clever, or profound thing to say. Not so. Now is the time to use a
second form of questioning—the *informational request
question.* The informational request question, unlike
the ritual question, is what it appears to be. When you
ask the question, you are doing so because you appreciate the fact that your partner in conversation probably
knows the answer, and you don't.

Again, many shy people stop at this point because
they feel that to request information is to admit ignorance. It is. Ignorance, however, is not stupidity. Ignorance means simply not knowing something (a quality
we're all rich in!), while stupidity means the inability to
comprehend something once it is explained. People are
almost always pleased and proud to have the opportunity to play the expert. When you ask me about something I know, and you don't, I feel good about myself,
and good about you for giving me the opportunity to
feel I know something. In addition, of course, I feel
pleased by your continuing interest in what I have to
say. I understand that it is logical and natural for you
not to know the answer to the question you're asking,
because you're asking about my thoughts, my feelings,

my experiences, my work, my life. Usually, I want to make contact as much as you do.

Some months ago, I attended a party given for one of my friends who was moving to another city. She is a journalist and most of her friends who attended the party were also journalists who mostly knew one another. I, on the other hand, knew only her. This situation brought on a relatively severe (for me) attack of situational shyness. I had butterflies, sweaty palms, and a general feeling of restlessness and nervousness. I got into thinking a set of negative thoughts: "I'm out of place here . . . They're not interested in me anyway . . . I'll bet they're all wondering who the turkey over here in the corner is." I began acting out my shyness: I sat in corners; I kept going to the bathroom or pretending I was freshening my drink; I didn't meet people's eyes, or smile, or volunteer any greeting or comment of my own.

I would like to report that I used the skills I know to overcome my own shyness, but that's not the way it happened.

At some point in the middle of the evening, a young woman sat down next to me, and began to talk with me.

SHE: "Hi, I'm Linda. Who are you?" (ritual question)

I: "Hi, Linda. I'm Art."

SHE: "How are you enjoying the party?" (ritual question)

I: "Okay, I guess. Well, to tell the truth, I'm feeling kind of out of it. I've never met anyone here, and I'm afraid I don't know much about journalism."

SHE: "So it sounds like you're feeling a bit out of your element, huh?" (active listening)

I: "Yeah." (long pause)

SHE: "What do you do, Art?" (ritual question)

I: "I'm a psychologist."

SHE: "How neat! What kind of psychology do you practice?" (information request)

I: "Clinical psychology. I talk to people about problems they're having in their lives."

SHE: "Oh—like, if I'm having trouble adjusting to a new job or person in my life, I might come to you for advice?" (active listening)

I: (warming up now) "Well, not exactly—I don't so much give advice as I work with people to help them understand their own feelings and what's really going on in the problem they're having."

SHE: "So it's not as if you tell them how to solve their problem." (active listening)

I: "That's right! What I usually find is that when a person really finds out how he feels about a problem, what to do about it sort of naturally comes clear."

SHE: "So you're really saying that the solution to the problem is there all the time." (active listening)

I: "Sure. Well, sometimes it turns out that somewhere along the line a person has just missed some essential bit of information or particular skill that can really help him out, but usually those things are easily learned once he or she has really gotten clear about the problem itself."

SHE: "You're saying then that advice is only an incidental part of what you do?" (active listening)

I:  "Well, in importance, yes, but in time, no. See, the really important part of psychotherapy, the defining of the problem and the exploring of the person's feelings about it, can often be done in just a few sessions. The learning of the skills part, which is also important, can take quite a long time."

SHE:  "You mean then that coming to understand how I feel about a problem is the most important part of therapy and that sometimes happens faster than learning the skills I need to overcome it. Is that right?" (active listening)

I:  "Exactly." (long pause)

SHE:  "What kind of problems do you treat, Art?" (information request)

Our conversation went on for quite some time. Linda's skillful use of ritual questions, active listening, and information requests had the overall effect of really promoting contact between us. The way she talked to me repeatedly conveyed the message, "I'm interested in what you have to say." As a result, I began to feel that I was not out of place at the party, that I was someone who had some thoughts and experiences that were of value, and that I and my life were important. I should mention that as I began to recover from my attack of shyness, I was able to use some of the same methods to make contact with Linda. Needless to say, I ended our conversation liking her very much.

Here are a set of guidelines for using ritual questions, active listening, and information-request questions. As you reach each rule, go back and see how Linda used it. Remember that these "rules" are not ironclad; they are only guidelines. With a surprisingly small amount of practice, you will become comfortable enough with these ways of talking so that you will instinctively know which to use at any particular time.

*Use a ritual question when:*

1. you want to "break the ice." You have never met a person before, but you want to get to know him.
2. you want to reestablish an old tie. If you haven't talked to someone for a long time, assume you don't know much about him.
3. what you've been talking about seems pretty well talked-out, and there is no "natural bridge" to a new topic of conversation.
4. your last ritual question has drawn a very brief response. Don't assume from a one-word answer that the person doesn't want to talk with you. He may be shy, too, or just may not have much to say in answer to your question. Ritual questions are a bit like fly casts; sometimes more than one is necessary before you "get a bite."

*Use an active-listening response when:*

1. the other person has given you a piece of his thoughts, feelings, or experience.
2. you think you understand what he's said, but you're not sure.
3. the other person has made an "iceberg" statement—nine-tenths of it is under the surface.
4. you sense that he has a lot of thoughts, feelings,

or experience wrapped up in what was just —
said and could really "get into it" if you'd invite it.

*Use an information-request question when:*

1.  any question, the more obvious the better, oc-
    curs to you. Give the other person a chance to be
    the expert.
2.  something said requires more technical informa-
    tion in order for you to understand it fully.
3.  something said leads you to believe the other
    person could shed some light on a question in
    your own life. Go ahead and ask. He'll be pleased
    to help.

Don't expect to put together a conversational style
like Linda's by tomorrow. It takes time and practice to
become a masterful listener. But a good way to begin
is to set a goal of making one ritual question, one active-
listening response, and one information-request question every day for a week. Carry a small notebook with
you to record the situation where you asked or made
each response. Briefly summarize how it worked out.
When you've successfully done each once a day for a
week, raise the ante to two or three a day. Soon these
ways of talking will become a normal part of your style
and you will find that you are making contact more
often and more deeply.

## Review

In this chapter we've had a chance to approach other people in new ways—signaling that we really do want contact. First, we focused on other people—on their needs and desires instead of our own. Keep working on this, remembering that the self-involvement you have learned as a shy person has kept you from noticing others and from giving anything of yourself.

The key to your new approach is *listening*. Make an effort to hear what others are really saying and to respond in a way that assures them you are interested. We call this *active listening*, and it provides you with a blueprint for making conversation without fear.

Finally, we examined ways to get a conversation started through ritual questions and questions that request information. With your new techniques and attitudes you are ready to begin participating in conversations rather than avoiding them. Good luck!

3 questions

# SIX

# Sending Nonverbal Signals

A NEW YORK CABDRIVER jams on his brakes as a car bearing Iowa license plates runs a red light on Forty-second Street. The cabbie's eyes bulge, he bites his lower lip, and then he stabs viciously upward with the middle finger of his right hand. He doesn't say a word, but his message could not be clearer if he shouted it.

A Hollywood starlet appears on a television commercial for mattresses. As she looks meltingly into the eye of the camera, she allows her tongue to protrude slightly between her teeth, and slowly slides it over her lips. Lying down on the mattress, she cants her hips forward and stretches as sensuously as a cat. Her message could not be clearer if she whispered it.

Both the cabbie and the actress are using nonverbal communication. In fact, all of us are constantly producing nonverbal signals that accompany our verbal communication. The posture of our bodies, the expressions on our faces, what we do with our hands—all of these things are "speaking" to others. In fact, they speak whether we are aware of them or not. The unconscious expression of moods and attitudes through physical gestures and signs has come to be known as "body language," a term made popular by Julius Fast in his book of that title (New York: M. Evans & Co., Inc., 1970). The cabbie and the actress *knew* what they were saying with their gestures, but the vast majority of people speak body language without realizing exactly what they're saying.

One purpose of this chapter is to look at the unconscious body language of people who are shy. Since shy persons often say very little, their body language becomes an important means of communication—a way in which others can get some small idea of what they are thinking. In the second part of the chapter we will explore ways in which you can use body language to communicate consciously.

### Your Unconscious Body Language

As a shy person, you have been holding, deep within yourself, a negative self-image, a feeling that you are essentially different from or inferior to other people. Since body language often expresses deeply ingrained attitudes, we might expect that you communicate this negative opinion about yourself in the way you act.

The most obvious way in which you signal people that you feel different or inferior is in the way you relate to space. We all behave as if the real boundaries of our bodies are not marked by our skin but extend instead as much as three feet in every direction. This surrounding area is "our" space. Shy people become uncomfortable when anyone infringes on this personal space and they carefully avoid entering the personal space of other people. If there is a group of people in a room, shy persons will stay at the far edge of the group rather than at or near the center. Whenever possible, they will find a corner or stand against a wall to "protect" as much personal space as possible. If shy persons want to cross a crowded room, they will almost always make a wide circle around any groups of people rather than pass through them. And they will walk with arms down, shoulders hunched, head bowed, and eyes on the floor, as if to say, "Excuse me, I really have no choice but to pass through your space, but I really don't mean to offend you. If you like, you can pretend I'm not here."

When you take a place at the outer edge of a group or separate yourself from it altogether, the message you transmit is, "Since I am inferior to the rest of you, I don't feel I have the right to occupy the same space." And when you huddle in a corner or against a wall, you are saying, "Please don't come and make contact with me—I'm afraid you'll discover how different I am."

Your physical behavior communicates much the same message. Trying to be as invisible as possible, you use as few gestures as you can because gestures attract attention. Your posture is generally "closed"—arms and/or legs crossed—and this signal discourages others from entering your space.

Eye movements are another important type of nonverbal communication. Shy people do not meet other people's eyes with any regularity. Apparently operating on the principle that the "eyes are the windows of the soul," they seem to want to avoid having others glimpse the difference or inferiority of their own souls.

While nonshy people meet the eyes of persons who speak to them, shy people steadfastly avoid the eyes of others, focusing instead on the floor, the ceiling, or the other person's hands.

Shy people also control their facial expressions carefully. If I am convinced of my inferiority or oddity, it makes real sense that I should provide you with as few clues as possible about what I am thinking or feeling. Maybe if I don't give any evidence to the contrary, you will think I'm normal even when I believe I'm not. I don't nod or otherwise indicate that I agree with you, because you might be pulling my leg, and then think how foolish I'd look! I don't indicate that I disagree, because you might call on me to defend my opinion, and naturally you'd outwit me in an argument. Even if I do disagree, you're probably right, since you appear to be surer, more confident, more right somehow in what you think and feel. I don't laugh or smile at your witticisms, unless you warn me that you're telling a joke, because you might be serious, and if I laughed I'd offend you. I dare not look surprised or curious at what you're saying because you might be talking about something that *everyone* knows about except me, and you'd discover how stupid I really am. All in all, the safest facial expression for me to adopt is no expression at all. My deadpan expression is another way to block you from making contact with me and thus discovering how different and inferior I am. I end up safe, undiscovered, uninvaded, and alone.

An interesting sidelight on the nonverbal signals of shy people is the effect they have on others. One of the most firmly established maxims of modern psychology is that "ambiguity creates anxiety." Have you ever spoken to a person who made no comment, gave no facial expression, and only stared at you as you spoke? The longer he continues to give no indication of what he thinks of you or of what you are saying, the more your stomach tightens, the more your feeling of uneasiness grows, the more your need increases to get some reaction, any reaction. You begin to look questioningly at him as you talk. If he does not respond, you begin to leave open-ended gaps in the conversation, inviting him to respond. If he still gives no response, you ask him a direct question. And if he still refuses to respond, your anxiety grows to nearly unbearable proportions. At this point, you will begin to look for some way out of the situation. Your reaction to this person is approximately the reaction that many people have to someone who is painfully shy.

By avoiding physical closeness, by displaying closed and withdrawn physical postures, and by giving little or no facial indication of thoughts or feelings, the shy person creates an ambiguous situation for others, and they become anxious. Most shy people are not even aware that their behavior makes others uncomfortable. Typically, they are so preoccupied with their own fear that they fail even to notice what effect they have on others. The other person will often press a bit harder for some response from the shy one by pausing to invite a response or by looking more frequently into his eyes. This pressing, of course, only drives the shy one further into himself. The other person may then ask a direct question in an attempt to get a response. The shy one, thoroughly ill at ease now, answers as quickly and as briefly as possible. By this point, both people are so anxious and frustrated that they begin to look for a way out of the situation. The two part without having made any meaningful contact.

Nonshy persons often draw negative conclusions about themselves from this kind of encounter. None of us is totally free of the kind of negative ideas that dominate the mind of the shy person. When another individual seems not to want to be near us, when he or she leans or turns away from us, does not meet our eyes or smile, and offers no response to our conversational overtures, we begin to fear that we're stupid or silly or otherwise undesirable. It is in this way that painfully shy people may come to be regarded as "stuck up." Even though they behave the way they do because they're afraid, they seem to others to be superior, bored, cold, or rejecting.

### Learning to Use Nonverbal Signals

By this time, if you have been working at the exercises in the preceding chapters, you have begun to question the appropriateness of the negative subjective truths with which you have burdened yourself all these years. You have realized that many, if not all, of the negative ideas you held, even if they seemed true at the time you formed them, have remained true primarily because you had just "closed the file" on them. You are already taking steps to re-form your self-image and, as your idea of yourself becomes more positive, your actions will begin to show the change.

But some shyness behaviors may be maintained as

habits long after a person has successfully developed a nonshy self-concept. If a particular kind of behavior has been repeated often enough, it may persist even when its meaning is removed.

The rest of this chapter will suggest ways to break your old habits of nonverbal signaling and to use body language to transmit positive messages. You can learn to use nonverbal signals to let others know that you are interested in them and in what they feel and think. When you are able to convey these messages, other people will begin to react more positively to you.

How do we use body language to communicate these messages? Fortunately, laboratory research in the interests of improving counselor training has established a number of readily identifiable signals that transmit these messages. As we describe these signals, you will recognize them—confident, outgoing people you know use them often. And you will discover that these signals communicate very powerfully without a word being spoken.

The first of the signals involves the way you use your "body space." As a shy person, you have kept yourself spatially out of contact and have moved away from any potential contact situations. A first step in communicating that you are "open for contact" is to *move toward* the other person. A distance of three to six feet is necessary between people who are making initial contact. A distance greater than six feet will close off the possibility. So if you find yourself more than six feet away from someone you wish to talk to, don't be afraid to get up and move toward that person. The person will receive this message at an almost subconscious level as meaning, "I want to be closer to you."

The second message involves a change in what you do with your body once you are close enough to establish contact. Most shy people, in their desire not to be discovered or to intrude on the space of another, tend to pull up or lean back. Unfortunately, the other person often interprets the backward lean as an indication of disapproval or disinterest. When you are sitting, lean forward toward the person you are talking to. When standing, simply incline your head toward the person. When you alter your body position in this way, the message you are transmitting is, "I don't want to miss a word you're saying."

Another change involves the way in which you use your arms and legs. The average shy person tends to "cover up" physically by crossing arms or legs. He or she is imitating the turtle that pulls into its shell at the approach of danger. As you think about it, you may realize that "covering up" has become a very strong habit for you. It may feel awkward at first to remain physically "open" for any period of time. Be assured, however, that your open posture presents a very strong nonverbal message to others that says, "I am open to what you have to say. Please share yourself with me."

Another highly important way in which people relate to one another is by touch. Pediatric researchers have found that newborn babies can become seriously ill and even die when they are not sufficiently touched and fondled. If you are like most shy people, you have actively avoided touching other people or being touched by them, because you have intuitively known that touch is a very powerful way of making contact. Now that you have begun to change the negative ideas behind your fear of contact, you can begin to use touching as a powerful nonverbal message. Some kinds of touching convey specific meanings. An arm around the shoulders or waist indicates companionship. Using both hands to shake hands suggests warmth. Touching a seated person's knee with a finger serves to get his attention, while an open hand placed on the knee is a sign of affection. At first you may have to fight off the mistaken notion that touching another person is an intrusion of his or her space. Give yourself permission to take the risk. Go ahead and touch, and within a short period of time the increased warmth you feel from others will have erased your fears.

A third group of nonverbal signals involves your face. The first and most important signal is eye contact. As I pointed out earlier, the shy person avoids meeting another person's gaze. To the other person, however, your avoidance of eye contact presents an almost impassable barrier to communication. Have you ever tried to talk with someone who would not meet your gaze? It seems he is ignoring you, avoiding you, or is utterly distracted by something else. If he persists in refusing to meet your eyes, you'll probably give up your attempt to make contact.

Adequate eye contact, on the other hand, is a powerful nonverbal signal of respect and attention. When you meet and hold another person's eyes you are telling him, "What you are saying is important to me." Making eye contact may cause you to feel uncomfortable at first. Naturally so, since years of habit have conditioned you to avoid it. A good way to train yourself to more consistent eye contact is to work into it by five-second intervals. At first try to hold the eyes of another person for five seconds at a time. When you feel quite comfortable with five seconds (as you will in a remarkably short time), try ten seconds, then fifteen, and so on.

Another powerful nonverbal signal is smiling. When you smile while listening to someone, the message you are transmitting is, "I am enjoying being with you." Shy people are typically tense and anxious, so it's no wonder they don't have much experience in smiling. But as your anxiety level decreases, practice smiling as often as you can when in social situations, except when the other person's subject makes it inappropriate. As you convey your enjoyment at being with other persons, you'll find that they will relax, become less fearful of you, and begin really to enjoy being with you.

Finally, you can transmit very powerful signals of interest and acknowledgment by nodding your head. Shy persons avoid expressing nonverbal agreement with another's statements because they fear they may be called upon to defend the view they're agreeing with. Head-nodding, smiling, and other facial expressions (frowning, concentrating, looking disgusted, raising the eyebrows in surprise) are ways of being responsive to the communications of another person. Don't be afraid to feel along with the speaker and let your feelings show. This is the nonverbal equivalent of active listening. When others observe you nodding, smiling, and being otherwise responsive to them, the signal is clear: they know that they are being carefully and attentively listened to. When you nod, you are not saying,

"I agree"; you are saying, "Yes, I hear what you're saying and I think I understand."

By now you may be realizing that there is nothing magical or mystical about improving your communications with others. Verbal and nonverbal skills can be learned and perfected through practice. People not born in France can learn to speak French, but they have some study and catching up to do. Like the beginning language student, you need to catch up, too, and you can do it through study and practice. You may feel a bit awkward as you begin to practice your new skills in public. But all my experience with shyness suggests that your ease and "fluency" will develop with surprising speed.

An added bonus is that you will find that performing these new nonverbal maneuvers reduces your tension and anxiety in social situations. It is true that nonverbal signals are produced by internal thoughts and feelings. But the reverse is also true—performing the appropriate nonverbal gestures will help change your feelings about yourself. You can demonstrate this for yourself. Make a fist, tighten the muscles of your arm, clench your teeth, and begin to breathe heavily. Within moments you will find yourself thinking of something that makes you angry. Nonverbal behaviors can produce very real feelings. As you begin to use the nonverbal signals of liking and respect and attentiveness described in this chapter, you will find yourself feeling more and more "connected" and in contact with other people around you.

## Exercises

The secret of nonverbal signaling lies not in the specific meaning conveyed in any one signal, but in the tremendous communicative power of such signals as a group. The problem in practicing them effectively is how to practice them together. No one of the signals is difficult to perform by itself, but many folks I have worked with tell me it is something of a trick even to remember all the signals when they are actually involved in a contact situation.

You can use the letters of the word SOFTEN as a way of jogging your memory to each one of the important nonverbal signals.

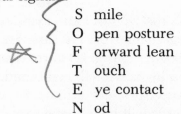

S   mile
O   pen posture
F   orward lean
T   ouch
E   ye contact
N   od

Close your eyes and run through the list several times. Later during the day, review the word SOFTEN. You will find that five or six repetitions will set the list firmly in your mind.

*Exercise 1.* Turn on your radio or TV to a talk show (even a news broadcast will do, although they are usually too fast for our purposes). Now turn up the volume so that you can hear every word clearly while you sit in front of a mirror.

Imagine that you are with the person who is talking, perhaps at a cocktail party or having coffee. When you feel you have the thread of what he is talking about, think to yourself "SOFTEN" and begin to run through the checklist, using each signal in order. See how many times you can go through the entire list in ten minutes. At first, you may be able to do it only once, but after a few sessions with your radio or TV you will find that you can SOFTEN five, six, or even ten times or more during the ten-minute period.

*Exercise 2.* When you have practiced the SOFTEN checklist enough to be at home with it, you can begin to use it with other people. Use the checklist once on the first day. As soon as you meet this goal, raise the ante to twice in one day, then three times, and so on. By the time you are SOFTENing your behavior five times a day, you will find that the signals and gestures are becoming an easy and natural part of your behavior.

*Exercise 3.* After two weeks of practicing the SOFTEN checklist, experiment with yourself to prove the power of these signals. Deliberately reverse them. Once, twice, or three times (enough to satisfy your curiosity), consistently *do the opposite* of every signal on the checklist. Don't smile. Close your posture. Lean back and away. Don't touch. Look anywhere but at the person's eyes. Don't nod or give any head signal that you are listening.

Now watch the effect that your old characteristic behaviors have on people. They become anxious and uneasy. They fumble for words. They ask questions. In a short period of time, they find a reason to break off the contact. When you try this, you will become very aware of the effect your nonverbal signaling has had on people for much of your life.

Reverse use of the SOFTEN checklist can play an occasional but highly useful role in discouraging people whom you are quite sure you don't want to talk to. Women will find that reverse SOFTENing very successfully fends off unwanted approaches from men. These signals also discourage all but the most aggressive sales people.

Several clients to whom I've introduced the SOFTEN checklist have worried that they will use the signals inappropriately and appear foolish. Don't worry. There are only a few rules to remember, which you are unlikely to violate anyway.

1. Don't SOFTEN if you don't want contact.
2. Don't smile if the other person is telling you something sad or painful.
3. Don't touch in a sexual way if you are not inviting sexual contact.

Remember that the problem in the past has not been your inappropriate use of the SOFTEN signals. You haven't been using them at all. Push yourself now to use them as much and as often as you can. In time, your command of the signals will increase so that you will be using them with the precise timing that the concert pianist uses to touch the keys. There is nothing sacred about the order of the SOFTEN checklist—it is only a convenient device for remembering and practicing all the signals. As you become more comfortable with the signals, feel free to mix and match them to your taste. Once you are comfortable with them, the only rule is *do them*—as often as possible—and enjoy the rapid increase in the quality of your contact with others.

# SEVEN

# How to Tell Others Who You Really Are

WE HAVE SPENT CONSIDERABLE TIME exploring ways you can give other people the love, attention, respect, and acceptance they seek from contact with you. Give these things, and chances are that those who receive them will grant you the same things in return. Viewed in this way, all successful relationships can be seen as a form of mutual pleasuring.

So far we have discussed some ways in which you can show your willingness to give. They include active listening and the SOFTEN nonverbal signals. But these techniques, effective as they are, provide only half the ingredients of a full, meaningful relationship. They are the path by which you can enter the world of another person, but they do relatively little to disclose *you*: your experience, your thoughts, and your feelings.

Genuine contact is a two-way street. You must want to gain entry to the experience of others, but you must also be willing to let others enter your world of experience. Without providing such entry, the skills we have discussed so far are incomplete at best. If you constantly encourage other people to reveal themselves, but provide no opening for revealing yourself, the others will finally feel that they have been duped, enticed into showing their hand while you pull your cards closer to your chest. They have trusted you, but you have refused to trust them.

Genuine contact requires of you a greater gift than the gifts of attention and acceptance that we have already discussed. It requires that at some point you give something of yourself. You do this by learning to tell about your thoughts, your feelings, and your experiences. When you give of yourself, you make the ultimate statement of respect and acceptance of the other person.

The idea of self-disclosure, letting another person in on who you really are, is a frightening idea for most shy people. In this reaction they are not alone. All of us are more or less afraid to expose ourselves as we really are, without shame, pretense, or facade. When we do so, we put ourselves in the position of leaving it to others to decide whether to accept or reject us.

We all want and need to be loved. And we learn very early that love is in the hands of other people. Beginning with our parents, we learn that other people can give or withhold love as they choose. They may reward us with approval and love when we please them and punish us with disapproval and rejection when we displease them. So we learn to do what they like in order to "earn" their love. Sometimes we even try to *be* what they think we should be.

Some folks are instant analyzers of people, making rapid and uncannily accurate estimates of what another person is looking for. Then they portray the character they judge will please the other. They can be charming, witty, deferential, flattering, even sarcastic and cutting, depending on what the situation calls for. These folks are the active deceivers—they please others by pretense and ingratiation.

Shy people, on the other hand, develop more passive but no less effective methods of deception. Early on, shy people seem to understand the principle of the psychologist's ink-blot test: Given a very indefinite picture, people will see just what they want to see. So when a shy person takes a low profile, says little, makes few nonverbal signals, seldom states an opinion, and never lets his or her feelings show, people will often "fill in the blanks" with whatever qualities please them most. Like the active deceiver, the shy person is saying, "If you see in me what pleases you, maybe you will accept me."

This type of evasion is not easy. To give little or no indication of the real nature of one's feelings day after day is a task requiring the skill and delicacy of a bullfighter. For the shy person, stepping into social situations can be as perilous as stepping into the bullring for the matador. The shy individual must face the advances of others; and, with the subtlest of twirls of the cape of evasion, cause the threat of contact to pass without penetrating the vitals of his or her being. The shy person believes that such a penetration would result in rejection as surely as the penetration of the bull's horns would result in the death of the matador.

Given this situation, shy people see themselves in a very unpromising human dilemma. On the one hand, they think, they can settle for the shallow kind of contact that is achieved by putting on a facade to please another. On the other, they can choose to live with their loneliness and the conviction that they are essentially unlovable.

Fortunately there is a third choice: the decision to give up the idea that you are different, inferior, unlovable—and take the risk of disclosing a part of your real self to others. It is not an easy thing to do, but it is the path to real and satisfying relationships.

At times, of course, our fear of self-disclosure is a useful safeguard. It would be unwise, for instance, for military recruits to attempt to establish contact with their drill instructor based on disclosure of their real feelings toward him. Similarly, it is probably not the better course for most of us to offer a full and complete disclosure of our feelings toward our jobs to our boss in hopes of establishing a fuller relationship with him.

But the problem of most shy persons is that they extend their fear of self-disclosure inappropriately to others in their lives. We are all guilty of this at times, setting up our friends or acquaintances as our parents, our drill instructors, our bosses, our judges. We assume that they demand that we feel certain feelings and think certain thoughts. Almost every shy person I've ever worked with has had a vague but impossibly exaggerated idea of what other people expected of him or her.

As we husband our thoughts, revealing them to no one, they seem to us to become stranger and stranger. We finally persuade ourselves that we must be the only ones in the world to feel the things we feel.

I recall an encounter group that I led a few years ago.

During one session I asked each person to express a fear he or she had. After several people had talked about their personal fears, the group's attention turned to Jerry, a twenty-nine-year-old graduate student who was one of the quieter members. Jerry was married, the father of two children, and was expecting to complete his graduate program in engineering within the year. With his eyes on the floor, obviously struggling to control tears, he explained to the group that since his early adolescence he had experienced occasional feelings of sexual attraction to several male acquaintances. Once in a while, while masturbating, he had fantasies of having sex with them. Although he had never acted on these feelings, he confessed to a deep fear that he might be a "latent homosexual."

The group's reaction to this disclosure took Jerry by surprise. Joe, a varsity basketball player, told about the time he'd gotten an erection during a locker-room wrestling episode in high school. Wynn described how the mutual masturbation "club" he'd been a member of during junior high had awakened him to the experience of sexual pleasure. Sally stated that she occasionally indulged in lovemaking with another woman as a "change of pace" from heterosexual activities, while remaining quite sure that men were the main focus of her sexual interest. Several other members of the group mentioned that while they had no real interest in exploring the activity in reality, they too had occasional homosexual fantasies.

Jerry summarized his feelings through tears of relief when he said, "For years now I've never told anyone about these feelings because I was afraid they would recoil in disgust. I've believed that I was sick and perverted. I feel closer to all of you because I took a risk and let you know something about my inner feelings, and not only did you accept them, but it turns out that many of you even feel some of the same things." Turning to me, he said, "I guess for the first time I really feel as if I'm a part of this group."

Sometimes we hang our fear of being rejected on the other person by assuming that he or she will be hurt or upset by what we think or feel. Cynthia and Andy, married only seven months, came to me for help because of a strange pattern that had emerged in their sexual relationship. Although many evenings at home had an intimate and romantic beginning, giving rise to an increasing sexual excitement, actually going to bed seemed to click an "off" switch in Andy's interest in sex, and the couple most often went to sleep frustrated and unfulfilled.

I asked them to give me a detailed description of a normal evening in which the upsetting event might happen. Taking turns, they painted a picture that struck me as the lovely kind of romantic interlude that newlyweds seem able to create. At some point in their narrative, Cynthia said, with some embarrassment, "I have this cute little thing I always say on the way to bed, like 'Mama's really gonna make her little boy happy tonight.' "

As she related this part, I noticed a deep flush creeping up Andy's neck and, turning to him, I asked, "Does it turn you on when she says that?"

"I dunno," he replied, looking at the floor, "it's cute, I guess."

Sensing that something was amiss here, I asked Cynthia to tell Andy again that she really wanted to know how he actually felt. "To tell the truth," he responded, "—and please don't be offended, Honey—I just can't stand it when you say that 'mama' thing. I mean, I know you think it's cute, but, well, to me it sounds really goofy, it gives me kind of a creepy feeling. I keep hoping you won't say it, and you always do, and then I think, 'Oh God, she said it again,' and I get kind of irritated, and then I sort of lose my desire to make love."

Cynthia, with an expression of real surprise, replied, "I only say that because I thought you really liked it." When we explored the reasons Andy had never expressed his feelings about Cynthia's "cute" statement, he confessed that he was afraid that she would be hurt or offended. For the sake of avoiding possible hurt or offense (and avoiding his subconscious fear that she would reject him if he were honest about his feelings), Andy for months had sacrificed their experience of sexual contact. With this small misunderstanding out of the way, things were soon going beautifully for them.

Andy had fallen victim to a common belief that a person should not express his or her negative or "bad" feelings. This fear of the negative often springs from our early childhood training. Our parents react more positively to us when we are happy than when we are angry, and we come to believe that we are "bad" when we are angry or when we state our needs and preferences instead of being conventionally "nice."

When we deny someone entry into our world by refusing to disclose what we think is a "bad" feeling, we shut down an important channel of communication. And often, when we "nurse" the anger and keep it alive but hidden, it closes down other channels of communication as well. We find ourselves drifting out of contact with the other person altogether. Many married couples have had no significant contact for years, all beginning with a "bad" feeling one failed to communicate to the other.

A number of common conventions of our language reflect our avoidance and fear of self-disclosure. We have developed ways of speaking to others that make it seem we are in contact when, in fact, all we are doing is filling the air with words. Most of what we call conversation is in reality a clever system of verbal behavior that allows us to be together without making contact.

We learn, for instance, that normal social conversation should consist of impersonal ideas rather than personal feelings. We play such games as "my car–your car," "my dog–your dog," "my trip–your trip" long after the need for breaking the ice has passed.

Another language convention we learn in order to mask or prevent self-disclosure is what I call the "pronoun trick." You make a statement of your own thoughts or feelings, but instead of indicating that they are your thoughts or feelings by using the first-person pronoun "I," you use the second-person "you," or even (as is popular in Great Britain) the third-person indefinite pronoun "one." Very shy people often make their language clumsy and almost grotesque in their attempt to make a personal statement without attaching it to their own person. I have a transcript of an interview in which a patient said:

You feel like you can't just speak up every time your husband steps on your toes. I mean, you've spent years developing all your little routines around the house, and then just because you decide you don't like them, you don't uproot the whole family system. It seems like a person would be pretty unfair if she did that, wouldn't she?

How could I respond to such a statement? It seemed clear that she was talking about herself, yet her language suggested that she was talking about me—or at least about some vague unspecified group of people. Her use of the wrong pronouns clouded the feelings with which she was dealing, as if to say, "This is not really what I think and feel, it's just a general feeling that people have."

When you use the pronoun trick, you make an impossible demand that the other person deal with the thought or feeling you express without making contact with you, the thinker and feeler.

## How to Talk about Yourself

The process of achieving contact through self-disclosure is similar to the processes of changing the other shyness behaviors we have discussed. The first step is to identify the ways in which you do not make use of contactful behaviors. Compare your own ways of talking about yourself with the faulty patterns of self-disclosure we have described so far. The most basic question you can ask of yourself is, "Am I telling people anything about myself, however indirectly?" There are people who are so shy as almost never to make any comment about themselves. The person who falls into this category becomes a kind of mystery person to those around him. They are discouraged from trying to find out about him by his very silence. They begin to fear that if they ask directly, they will be quickly shot down. Such intimidation fits right into the shy person's subconscious intention to avoid contact. As you have discovered, however, it leaves the shy person terribly isolated and lonely.

If you recognize yourself among those who seldom if ever give any information about themselves, what should you do? The answer is to begin to tell others about yourself. The least scary way to begin to do so is at the level of pure information. Tell someone you know about your job. Describe a project on which you are working. Tell about a trip you've gone on. Don't expect your first disclosures to be polished or to achieve a sudden deep relationship with someone. That will come in time. First you must break your pattern of non-self-disclosure by talking—talking about yourself.

If you have maintained silence about yourself for years, you are likely to feel a certain amount of fear about telling the most simple story. Recognize that such fear is as natural as the fear you might feel before you jump from a diving board for the first time. The beginning diver overcomes his fear by doing it. Soon he learns that he will not be injured, and in a short time he becomes comfortable with diving. None of this could happen, however, if he did not perform the original leap. It is unrealistic to wait to tell someone something about yourself until you feel no fear. Only by disclosing yourself to another will you become more courageous.

I have found that the most common worry shy folks express is that they will bore people. Do you often feel bored when someone is sharing himself or herself with you? Of course you don't, and it's not because the other person has anything utterly fascinating to say. You feel interested because what he or she is saying represents an attempt to make contact. People are not interested in you for your entertainment value. They can get better entertainment than most of us can provide simply by turning on the TV. It is *you* that they are interested in, and contact that they seek. If you will let them in on who you are, no matter how banal, trite, or boring you may think yourself, you will be rewarded with the kind of contact you need and want. Remember, what may seem an everyday experience to you can strike a listener as fascinating; it happens more often than you think.

If you are satisfied that you do furnish others with adequate information about yourself, but somehow contact does not result, then it's time to examine the ways in which you provide that information. It may be that you have fallen into a pattern that fails to convey accurately what you think or feel.

The first question to ask is whether you censor what you reveal, talking only about your "positive" feelings and experiences. We all labor under our internal restraints to be "good" by not expressing our "bad" feelings. And the idea is reinforced by such common maxims as "If you can't say something nice, don't say anything at all."

Nonshy people have learned to take this type of advice with a large grain of salt. They understand that no one feels fine all the time, that no one finds everything agreeable, and that no one is always "nice." When you try to present a "too nice" picture of yourself to others, from fear of expressing negative feelings, you make all of your self-disclosure suspect. No one knows when you are telling the truth—or rather everyone knows you must not be telling all the truth.

Contact cannot be established with a pretend person. As soon as we cover over our "negative" feelings, we close off contact between ourselves and others. We develop all sorts of notions about the awful things that will happen if we are honest about our feelings. The truth is that failure to express them directly usually makes them worse, in the same way that holding down the lid on a steaming pot increases the pressure within. Conversely, letting others in on "bad" feelings often extends the contact and increases the possibilities that the angry feelings will be resolved. Chapters 9 and 10, on assertiveness, will follow up this idea.

A second question you should ask if your efforts at disclosing yourself seem unsuccessful is, how much of your self-disclosure really has to do with *you?* Remember that the reason for sharing your thoughts is to share yourself. If your conversation expresses ideas that seem to have little to do with yourself, your talk really becomes an evasion of self-disclosure.

I once counseled a medical secretary named Kate who was an extremely shy person. As she started to learn the process of self-disclosure, I encouraged her simply to share information about herself. When she came for her next appointment, she said she had tried telling several people about her job, but no one seemed very interested and certainly no real contact had developed from it.

I asked her to tell me about her job as she would if I were a stranger. Kate's reply sounded something like this:

> I'm a medical secretary. It's my responsibility to schedule patients for the doctor's appointments. I also compile information for insurance filings. Often, it's my responsibility to see that the patients are comfortable in the waiting room. It's an interesting job.

I pointed out that her description could have been given by almost any medical secretary. She saw that while it was a fairly accurate description it told the listener almost nothing about her. After working together for a while to make her description more self-disclosing, it sounded like this:

> I really like being a medical secretary. I had no idea before I took the job how tough a task it is to keep a doctor's schedule in order! He's kind of absentminded, and after I got the hang of scheduling it became sort of fun to mother him and make sure he's in the right place at the right time.
>
> I find the insurance work kind of a drag, but I know it's important. I never had medical insurance for myself before this job, and I'm sure glad I have it now. I don't know what I'd do if I developed a condition that involved thousands of dollars worth of treatment!
>
> The really interesting part is my contact with the

patients. Even though I don't know what goes on in
the examining rooms, I get really involved with some
of the folks—how they're feeling, and how their
families are, and such. I think, depending on how
well I do my job, that I can help the patients feel a
lot less uptight about seeing the doctor.

On the whole, I really enjoy my job.

You can see immediately that Kate's revised job description contains a real sharing of herself. By communicating her own personal thoughts and feelings
throughout, she gives her listener a number of open-
ings to share her world of experience and, in so doing,
to make contact with her.

A third check on your self-disclosure language is to
notice whether you're using the pronoun trick, that is,
substituting "you" or "a person" or the British "one" or
the cornpone "a body" when what you really mean to
say is "I." A sure way to correct this tendency is to use
sentences that begin with the word "I." Beginning with
"I" ensures that you won't lose the word, or slip and use
one of the contact-avoiding pronouns. If you will practice a bit, "I language" will become a stable part of your
speech habits very quickly, because people will reward
"I language" by relating to your self-disclosures much
more directly.

You should be aware, as you begin to disclose yourself
to others, that there is a time lag between the beginning of a new behavior and the beginning of new responses from other people. Occasionally a patient of
mine has become discouraged when, once he has made
his "dive" into self-disclosing behavior, other people

did not respond immediately. Because you have presented yourself to others as shy and non-self-disclosing for so long, you have conditioned them to respond to you that way. At first, others who have known you may react with surprise and some confusion when you disclose yourself to them. Or they may not even notice. You will find that the longer you have known a person, the longer it will take to discourage him from responding to you as a shy person. On the other hand, someone you meet for the first time will react to your self-disclosing statements as if you had never been shy at all. All in all, however, it takes an amazingly short period of time to decondition even your oldest acquaintances. With a little time and patience, disclosing yourself more openly, even to a friend or spouse of twenty years, will lead you into an experience of deeper contact, and that means a new joy and pleasure for both of you.

# EIGHT

# A Program for Self-Disclosure

SOME SHY PEOPLE are more capable of self-disclosure than others, although almost all find some difficulties in talking about themselves. The program that follows assumes that people with shyness problems fall into three somewhat arbitrary groups. To make maximum use of the program, decide which group describes you. Then examine the individual exercises listed under that group. Starting with the first, imagine yourself performing each exercise. When you reach the first one that seems difficult, or that you recognize as something that you seldom or never do, go to the exercise just before it and begin there.

Over a period of weeks or months, work your way from your starting point all the way to the last exercise under Group III. Use a notebook or cassette recorder to plan and rehearse how you will perform each exercise and to record how you felt and how other people responded.

## *Group I*

You are extremely shy and almost totally non-self-disclosing. You find it difficult to talk to other people at all, let alone to make self-disclosing statements. You have put off or avoided practicing any of the conversation techniques of Chapter 5 or the nonverbal signals of Chapter 6 because you fear that sooner or later you will be asked about yourself. You may be very socially isolated, or you may be a peripheral member of a group who will not ask that you open yourself up to them, or you may be in a relationship in which your partner covers over your extreme shyness with his or her ease and confidence.

For each of the exercises below, go through a two-step preparation before you actually do them. First, write out what you will say or speak it into a recorder. Rework what you have written or recorded until it contains as much self-disclosure as you can pack into it (using "feeling talk" and "I language"). Then practice it, in front of a mirror, or with your eyes closed, imagining the other person or persons.

1. *Introduce yourself.* Your name is one of the important elements of your identity. Disclosing it to others is a symbolic way of inviting them into your world. A good introduction should include three elements: a greeting, your name, and a self-disclosing identifier (something that tells others where you fit into their experience). For example:

> "Hi, I'm Martha Washington, George's wife."
> "Hello, I'm Mary Jones, your neighbor two houses down."

2. *Tell about your job.* Remember that the key here is to share yourself through your description of your work. I find that many folks reject this exercise because they feel their job is too dull to tell anyone else about it. The fact is that very few people, excluding divers for sunken treasure and private detectives of the TV variety, have jobs that are so intrinsically interesting that other people want to hear about them. What people want to hear about is you, and telling about your job is one excellent way to do it. Use "feeling talk" and "I language" liberally and your job description will become an important avenue of self-disclosure.

3. *Tell about a trip you've made.* Again, the object is not to provide a travelogue. Your friend can find a better one on TV, anyway. Don't tell about the place. Tell about *you* in the place.

4. *Tell a joke.* Shy people, in my experience, almost never tell jokes. I suspect that they avoid the natural "on-stage" position telling a joke puts them in. You don't have to be Johnny Carson to tell a joke. The idea is to share yourself with others by letting them in on your sense of humor. Naturally, therefore, the joke you learn to tell should be one that you particularly enjoy. Whether others enjoy it depends less on how good the joke is, or your style of delivery, and much more on whether you enjoy it.

5. *Describe a project you're working on.* It's unlikely your friends need or want a handicraft lesson, unless they ask for it. They do, however, want to know what you do with your spare time, and what turns you on about doing it.

## Group II

You get along reasonably well with ritual social behaviors, and you can function in discussions of a fairly impersonal nature. You have practiced the behaviors described in Chapters 5 and 6, and you find that you can handle personal talk as long as it's focused on the other person. You find that the process breaks down when it becomes appropriate for you to share yourself. You become tense and anxious, can't think of what to say, and become afraid you'll "spoil your image" somehow.

As with the exercises in Group I, go through the two-stage preparation of writing out or recording what you will say and practicing it in private before actually trying it out with another person.

6. *State a belief that is important to you.* We are urged by popular wisdom to avoid controversy in our talk with other people, and therefore we commonly avoid talking about our convictions. Yet talking about our beliefs only creates real controversy (disagreement is *not* controversy!) when we demand that the other person subscribe to the same belief. What you believe is an important key to who you are, and approached in that way your beliefs can become an important vehicle for sharing.

Remember that the idea is to share yourself. This means that your emphasis should be less on what you believe and more on what feelings and experiences lead you to believe what you believe. Emphasize "feeling talk" and "I language."

7. *Tell a story that makes fun of you.* Extremely shy people have a neurotic fear of being laughed at. Yet all

human beings have experiences in which they appear foolish. You can gain control over your fear of being laughed at, paradoxically, by setting up a situation in which your friends are laughing with you as you laugh at yourself. To get the most self-disclosure value from your story (and to make it funnier) be sure to include a description of what you misunderstood in the situation, your puzzlement about the events in terms of what you believed, and your embarrassment when you correctly understood.

8. *Talk about your hopes for the future.* In doing so, you let people know where you are by indicating where you're going. One patient rejected this exercise because he felt that if he talked about what he wanted to accomplish in life, and then failed to make it, he would look foolish in the eyes of his friends. People are not interested in compiling performance statistics on you. They simply want to know you. When you share your hopes and your dreams, you share a significant part of yourself.

9. *Share a significant event from your childhood.* Another important way to allow people to know you is to share the processes by which you became who you are. I could never understand why a friend of mine seemed so preoccupied with never doing anything out of the ordinary in a public place until she shared a significant part of her childhood with me. As the daughter of an international diplomat, she often accompanied her parents to top-level state dinners and receptions. She was often featured as an "American princess." Although she was only eight or nine years old, she felt that her parents expected her to behave in a way that would

be more appropriate to a twenty-five-year-old woman. The constant fear that she would embarrass her parents by doing something wrong lived on into the present whenever she was in public. When she told me about her experience, I understood her in a new way and the quality of our contact was enriched.

It is not an experience itself, however, that forms your personality, but your thoughts and feelings in reaction to the episode. Try to convey not only what the experience was, but also what it was like to be *you* having that experience.

10. *Tell about a fear that you have.* All of us have fears. To share them with another is to open ourselves to him or her at the deepest levels of our being. Revealing a point of vulnerability is an act of ultimate acceptance and trust. When you deliberately expose your fear to another person you are signaling that you trust that person not to hurt you. You also exorcise your fear by bringing it out of the dark closet of your mind into the light where you can see it for what it is.

Try to avoid the temptation to discuss your fear as a joke. Being afraid is not a laughing matter. Generally this exercise is most appropriately performed with one other person rather than with a group.

## Group III

You are rather comfortable in most social situations. Although you are not usually the one to initiate self-disclosure, you are able, if asked, to relate experiences like those in the exercises for Group II without too much difficulty, as long as the experiences you are relating are at a comfortable distance in space and time. But you become tense and anxious and lose the opportunity to make contact when the situation requires that you express what you are feeling here and now. You have difficulty expressing either positive or negative feelings directly to other persons. It is hard for you to express a preference that differs from the inclinations of others. You respond in a way you think will please them, even when this forces you to deny your own needs and wants.

As in the exercises for Groups I and II, first write out or record what you will say, then practice by yourself before actually doing it with another person.

11. *Express a preference.* Shy people often express their feelings of inferiority by leaving to others choices that they have the opportunity to make. The effect of their refusal to express a preference is to deny their companions knowledge of them through their tastes and habits. When another person asks, "Would you prefer this or this?" he is asking for entry to that particular part of your experience. When you reply, "Whatever you'd like," or "I don't care," you think you are being pleasing and deferential. In reality, you're refusing to open a door on which your friend has knocked. Far from being pleased, the other person may feel frustrated and even angry.

You will find, when choices are presented to you, that in many instances you have so successfully avoided your own feelings that you will actually feel no real preference. The way to break this pattern is to make a choice anyway.

You can use this exercise either when a choice is

given to you (as in "Would you like to do this or this?")
or when a proposal is made and you can think of something you would rather have or do. Use "I language"—
"I'd like" or "I want"—and remember that the other
person is no more obligated to follow your preference
than you are to follow his or hers.

12. *Tell someone something you like or admire about
him.* Shy people usually do not provide positive responses to others because of a curious projection of
their own feelings onto others. They know that they
feel uncomfortable to have the attention of other people on them, even when that attention is positive and
approving. So they assume other people feel the same
way. From a desire not to make others uncomfortable,
they avoid making positive comments to them. The
effect of this silence is often to raise the anxiety of those
around them because the others can't tell if their behavior is pleasing or obnoxious to the shy person.

The way to perform this exercise is to use the following sentence model:

"I really like the way you _____. It makes me
feel _____."

Such comments are far more effective when made at
the moment you become aware of liking the other person. "Saved-up" responses, days or weeks later, may
sound stale.

13. *Tell someone about something he or she does that
you don't like.* The reasoning behind this exercise and
the directions for it are the same as those for number
12 above. It's a little bit harder to do, however, because
we have all been trained not to express our negative
feelings. When you hold back your negative feelings,

though, you deny yourself and your friend an important area of contact. You may also be setting up a time bomb that may explode much later (in the form of anger that has been long repressed) and damage or destroy your relationship.

Use "I language" with this exercise. You have no right to tell someone else that his or her behavior is wrong, silly, stupid, or obnoxious. All that you can say legitimately is that you don't like it. Use "feeling talk" to describe why you don't like it.

14. *Tell someone that you like (or care for, or love) him or her.* A simple statement of affection is one of the most powerful combinations of attending and self-disclosure we can communicate. You convey all the attending signals of respect, attention, warmth, and acceptance, and at the same time you disclose your own innermost feelings.

This exercise is subtly different from numbers 12 and 13. This time you are not telling your friend about his or her behavior, but about the total effect he or she has on you. A good format for this exercise is very much like 12 and 13: "John, I really like you very much. When I'm with you, I feel very free and full of life."

## How to Mix Self-Disclosure with Listening

I've pointed out that contact is a two-way street. Chapters 5 and 6 contain some "street signs" to point you toward the other person. They are the means by which you convey trust, respect, liking, warmth, and acceptance for other people. Chapters 7 and 8 provide some ways to point the other person toward you. Self-disclosure is the second direction of the two-way street. You are saying, "Here I am if you wish to come in my direction."

When you approach another person with the idea of making contact, it is your responsibility to move in his or her direction, using questions, active listening, and nonverbal signals to communicate your interest. Once you have established your interest in the other person, you begin to indicate your willingness to share your experience. You do this by making an occasional reference to yourself (perhaps a comment about your job, your hobby, your family). These indications open "doors" into your experience and are invitations to the other person to enter your world.

If the other person is neither a bore nor excessively shy, a response will usually come fairly soon—if not immediately—in the form of a question about something you have said. In my own case, I sometimes mention my dogs, who represent an important part of my experience. If the person I'm talking to wants to enter my world through that door, he or she will often ask, "What kind of dogs do you have?" When this kind of response occurs, the nature of the conversation changes—now the other person is listening to you, and expressing his or her interest and attention. Sooner or later, he will make another "invitation" to his own experience and, if you accept, the conversation shifts again. A two-way street has been established, and with each shift the conversation becomes more contactful and satisfying.

Two kinds of people will not respond readily to your offers to disclose something about yourself. We have already mentioned the bore. He responds to your attention as if he had stumbled across his own personal stage complete with an admiring audience. He will milk you endlessly for your attention while remaining quite unresponsive to your invitations into your experience. After you have issued a number of these and have no doubt of his unresponsiveness, you will probably conclude that making contact with him is not worth the effort. If he is very important to you, however, you may choose to confront him with his self-centered behavior.

A second type who may seem unresponsive to your sharing of yourself is another shy person. Shy people will be too preoccupied with their own internal monologues to pursue your invitations to contact. Of course, they are responsible for their behavior and its consequences, just as you are for yours, but you may wish to bend over backward to make them feel at ease. If you wish, you can share some of the problems you have had with shyness. Or you may wish to continue with your attending behaviors long after you would normally expect contactful responses, knowing that it takes a good deal of extra assurance for a shy person to feel that it is safe to make contact.

The processes of attending and self-disclosure are like the two halves of an electrical circuit. When connected, they will result in the free flow of shared experience between two people, and that is genuine contact.

# NINE

# Assertiveness: Standing Up for Your Rights

SHY PEOPLE approach life with the basic sense that they are different from or inferior to the vast majority of other human beings. Their conscious expressions of these negative attitudes usually include a tendency to judge themselves very harshly—and a basic unwillingness to stand up for their rights.

An important consequence of shy people's harsh and unrealistic judgments of themselves is the habit of granting a kind of superiority to everyone else. They consistently place the preferences and demands of others above their own because they are convinced that other people have a better claim to personal happiness than they do.

Shy people don't believe the words of the Declaration of Independence, that ". . . all Men are created equal, [and] they are endowed by their Creator with certain unalienable Rights; [among which] are Life, Liberty and the Pursuit of Happiness. . . ." The shy person thinks that other people have these rights but he's not so sure about himself. He considers himself a nonentity without rank, privilege, or rights.

If you have read this far, you have taken some steps toward changing your fixed negative ideas about yourself; and you are beginning to act as if more positive and helpful ideas are true. As the new self-image begins to develop, you should begin to treat yourself as an individual with the full rights you accord to other people. You should be granting yourself a wider latitude to be the person you are and you should be willing to encounter others with full awareness that you are a psychological equal.

But these changes will not happen automatically. Your habit of being nonassertive has been developed over many years, and habits can be tyrants. Normally, habits are enormously helpful in simplifying our daily lives. How complex things would be if we had to make a separate decision about every act we performed! Habits govern our routine behavior and free us to concentrate on more important issues in life; they are a kind of automatic pilot.

Your habit of nonassertiveness, however, was formed at a time when you had your old negative beliefs about yourself. An automatic pilot was set, but you were headed in the wrong direction. Now you have decided to change the direction of your life, and that means that you must make a strong, conscious effort to break the habits that were designed to keep your life on its old course.

Assertiveness is simply behaving as if you have the right to be who you are. That sounds absurdly simple until we notice how much of our behavior represents a denial of that right. We permit others to draw on our time and energy when we really don't want to give it, in the hope that they will repay the debt with a bit more love. We pay lip service to attitudes and beliefs that are not really ours because we're afraid we'll be rejected if we disagree. We go along with the plans and agendas of others because we are afraid to seem wet blankets or bad sports. How cheaply we sell our birthrights of personal identity for a spurious kind of acceptance that is based on a denial of who we really are!

Behaving assertively is a way of declaring our right to think what we think, feel what we feel, believe what we believe, want what we want, enjoy what we enjoy. As such, it is a special form of self-disclosure. When we behave assertively, we reject our old insecure tendency to behave only in ways we believe will cause others to like us, and instead we take the risk to openly be ourselves and leave to others the choice of whether to like us. Assertiveness differs from the more general kinds of self-disclosure discussed in Chapters 7 and 8, primarily in its goal. General self-disclosure, by opening our own world of inner experience to another, has contact as its goal. The particular kind of self-disclosure that we call assertiveness is aimed at establishing and defending our right to have that inner experience in the first place.

The personal effects of nonassertive behavior on both the shy and the nonshy person are devastating. To the extent that we do not use our inalienable right to make choices about our own lives, we lose control over the circumstances of our existence. We close ourselves into a behavioral closet walled by the intentions and agendas of other people. The emotional impact of this loss of control over our lives is depression, often rather severe. When we realize the power we have given away to the other people in our lives, we feel frustrated and angry with them. Then we sink into a tight-lipped silence, or we eventually explode in a hostile and destructive outburst that comes as a complete surprise to others, who before our outburst had no indication of our real feelings.

Martha Morton was a fortyish suburban housewife who had quite literally become a prisoner in her own home. She came to therapy because she realized that there was nothing in her daily activities that she would choose to do if she did not feel that she had to. She got up at six each morning to prepare a series of breakfasts timed to the schedules of her husband and four teen-aged sons. By eight thirty she was on her way to her job as a toll-taker on the freeway, a job she hated but felt forced to keep in order to help make ends meet. By two thirty she was on her way back home to try to repair the damage from breakfast, clean the house, and begin preparing dinner. After dinner she cleaned up the dishes, and then helped her youngest with his homework (her husband, Herb, was usually too tired). She usually had time for an hour or so of TV before bed at ten.

To her sons, Martha was a nameless household functionary. Since she was a very shy person, she had relatively little verbal interchange with them, tacitly leaving most of the interpersonal issues involved in parenting to Herb. They were all boys anyway, and "Herb would understand them better." The only times they did notice her was when a pair of pants wasn't pressed or a meal was late.

To Herb, Martha was an insoluble puzzle. He was

aware that she was drinking heavily and increasing her intake almost daily. Her face was a silent scream of depression. More and more often now, she was refusing his sexual overtures. His initial concern for her was rapidly turning into frustration and rage. He would ask, "What's wrong, Honey?" and she would reply, "Oh, nothing," sighing deeply and turning her face away. From Herb's perspective, of course, it was hard to imagine what she wanted of him. He was going out every day, working hard, providing a living and a home for the family.

For Martha, life was an unending marathon of despair. She had surrendered almost every claim she had to live her life in a way that was satisfactory to herself in favor of the demands of the others in her life. It did not occur to her that she had the right to say no. Herb, after all, was brighter than she was, had had more schooling, held a more responsible job; his need for her support was justified. The boys, she said, also had important tasks to perform in life, like completing their schooling, establishing relationships with girls, preparing for a good future. In her view, every other person in her family had a better right to live happily than she.

Although Martha was an eloquent defender of the validity of her husband's and sons' demands on her time and energy, nevertheless she was angry. Her nonassertiveness was a way of avoiding any direct verbal statement of her angry feelings, but her increased drinking, her sexual unresponsiveness, and her martyred sighs were clear statements of her inner rage. She knew she could not be angry with Herb and the boys; they were only taking advantage of a good thing. She wasn't angry with herself, be-

cause it only seemed right, given who she was, that
she should be doing what she was doing. She was just
angry with the way things were. Her impotent anger
plunged her into a very deep and consistent state of
depression.

Depression is not just a general "low" feeling; it is a
response to the belief that there is "no exit"—no way
to avoid or change a long-term situation that causes
pain or unhappiness. Dr. Martin Seligman of the University of Pennsylvania confirmed this in his animal
research laboratory. In the first stage of the experiment, the researchers constructed a cage divided in
half by a low barrier. The floor of one half of the cage
was electrified, while the floor of the other half was not.
Experimental rats were then placed one at a time in the
electrified part of the cage. When they were given a
shock, they screeched and leaped randomly about the
cage until one lucky jump took them over the barrier
to the nonelectrified part of the cage. In later trials the
rats learned to jump the barrier more and more quickly
to avoid the unpleasant shock.

In the second stage of the experiment, the barrier
was raised so that it completely divided the two halves
of the cage. Now it was impossible for the rats to escape
the shocks. As they learned that there was no escape,
a curious change came over them. Their panic subsided
and they became listless and showed little interest in
their surroundings. Eventually some even went to
sleep. The rats in the "no exit" situation were showing
the classical signs of depression in humans—lack of activity, lack of interest in their surroundings, with-

drawal, and excessive sleeping. In Martha's case she also drank alcohol to help her forget her apparently hopeless situation. The big difference, of course, is that for Martha there was a way out, as we will see.

When two assertive people interact, they can enjoy contact even when their needs, wishes, and plans contradict each other. They may negotiate a compromise, agree to defer temporarily the immediate needs of one to the needs of the other, or agree amicably to disagree and part ways. In any case, however, they have achieved a high level of contact—that is, a mutual sharing of inner experience.

But when one person in a relationship is not appropriately assertive, there is often trouble ahead. The assertive partner states his or her needs, desires, or plans openly and directly. If the request contradicts the needs or wishes of the nonassertive person, he or she will acquiesce anyway from fear of rejection. This is the first break in the flow of communication between the two. The nonassertive partner becomes angry because in complying with the wishes of the other he or she has violated his or her own desires. This anger leaks out (since the nonassertive person is afraid to express it directly) in the form of withdrawal or of an unconscious sabotage of the other's plan (the nonassertive partner agrees to cook breakfast, for example, but burns the bacon and undercooks the eggs). He or she may also make the assertive partner pay later in the form of guilt. Eventually, if the pattern of unwilling compliance continues, the hidden anger is expressed by depression. One partner has gone "underground" with his or her inner feelings, and contact is lost.

This loss of contact is clear in Martha's case. When she met Herb, she was powerfully attracted by his easy confidence and his carefree, happy-go-lucky approach to life. Not a particularly introspective person himself, he made few demands on her to disclose much of her inner feelings. He was forceful and straightforward with merchants and service people, successful and well-liked in his work, and he established social relationships quickly and easily. When he proposed marriage, his open arms seemed to her a perfect place for a shy person like herself to achieve safety from the more threatening aspects of life.

As their marriage progressed, she relied more and more heavily on Herb to run interference between her and life. He selected their home. He made major purchases and dealt with service people. He set up their social engagements. In return, she kept a clean and attractive household, served his meals, and bore him four sons in rapid-fire succession. But as the size and demands of the family grew, she became increasingly aware that the price of her safe harbor, in coin of time, energy, self-respect, and happiness, was greater than she had ever foreseen. Her protected niche had become a prison cell.

How could Herb have any idea of Martha's feeling? On the surface their life together was the way it had always been, only better. She'd always been happy keeping house and taking care of him and the boys. Her job, which she'd taken during a period between jobs for him, was probably a good change of pace for her. Once they'd been financially stable again he'd told her to quit if she wanted, but she'd told him it was okay and he certainly couldn't object to the extra money. Yet something was certainly bugging her. It seemed like the more he asked, the more she wouldn't talk about it. Well, if she couldn't or wouldn't say what the problem was, there wasn't much he could do about it. All the same, she sure wasn't much fun to be around. Sometimes he felt as if he didn't even know her.

It took Martha some time in therapy to realize that, unlike Seligman's experimental rats, she did have some choices. That awareness came in several distinct stages. First she had to deal with the negative elements of her self-image that led her to believe she deserved no better. She had so ignored her own needs and wishes that it required a long time for her to envision precisely what she did want. Finally she could make a list of these desires: (1) a greater sense that the family respected and cared about her; (2) more contact with the boys, and particularly with Herb; (3) relief from the sole responsibility for household chores; and (4) some time exclusively for herself.

Next she had to accept the fact that *she* was responsible for obtaining happiness for herself—not Herb, not the boys, not her therapist. This meant that she would have to bring her needs and wants to their attention. When she came to the point of assuming responsibility for herself, she was ready to learn that particular form of self-disclosure called assertiveness.

Martha decided that the first of her goals would be achieved if she could successfully accomplish the other three. Toward achieving a greater degree of contact with Herb and the boys, we began working on verbal and nonverbal contact skills—questioning and active listening and the SOFTEN signals. She began to ask the boys how school was going, and she found that as she communicated real interest in them, they opened up more and more to her and began to treat her like an important person in their lives. Herb melted like a snowball in the sun under her attention, for which he'd been starved for so long, and their sexual activities became more frequent as a natural result of their improved contact.

Having moved back into a position of communication with the family, Martha had to confront the issue of housework. To accomplish this involved much more self-assertion than Martha was accustomed to, and she found the idea rather frightening. Together, I playing the roles of Herb and the boys, we rehearsed the way that she would present the issue to them. It took some practice for her to learn to be assertive (telling about her feelings) without being aggressive and judgmental (telling them what was wrong with their behavior), and to limit her decision-making to decisions that were hers to make (saying what she would or would not do, rather than trying to compel them to do what she wanted). It came out sounding like this:

> I know that for a long time now I haven't been a very fun person to be with, for any of you, and I feel that it's way past time for me to share with you what's been going on inside me. You are my family, and maybe you can help me change some of the things that have been so wrong.
>
> I feel like a prisoner in my own family, mostly because of the way that I've chosen in the past to try

to do everything that anyone wants without giving any consideration to my own welfare. You see, I've felt, deep down, that the only way any of you would really care about me is if I took care of all your needs and wishes. Well, for my own good, I'm going to stop that. If it turns out that you love me in spite of that, fine. If not, it's still what I have to do for my own good.

From now on I'm going to make one breakfast every morning. It goes on the table at seven o'clock. I'll clean up the kitchen later in the day if each of you has rinsed and stacked your breakfast dishes. If not, I don't start dinner until you have.

I also need help from you with the other housework. There are a million ways we can work it out, and I'd feel good if we could work it out together. I've decided, even though I really like a neat, clean house, that if you won't help, neither will I.

I'm going to find some things to do that are only for me. Chances are those things will take up some of my time. I really hope that you all can adapt to my new schedule, as it develops, just as I've adapted to yours.

I know all this will mean some changes in the way we've always lived, but I believe they're right changes for me. I know that I can't keep doing what I've been doing. The way I've been living has been making me depressed and unhappy, and when I'm that way, I can't be much of a mom to you guys, or much of a wife to you, Herb, or, most important of all, much of a person to myself.

The results of this family conference were a big surprise to Martha. She expected Herb and the boys to be upset and angry. Instead, her thirteen-year-old's response was "Far out, Mom!" Herb was a bit more articulate. "So this is what's been eating you for these last few years?" he asked. "For a while, I thought it was me. I was wondering when you were going to file the papers! I guess, what with my job and all, I've never really thought about how hard you work. I'm not sure I'm going to like doing housework, but I know I really like it when you're halfway happy, and I really like it when you're at least talking to us."

Together, the family evolved a system they could all live with. The boys learned to cook and each made dinner once a week. Martha cooked two big meals a week, and Herb agreed to take them all to dinner on Saturday. Each boy agreed to take responsibility for one household chore, and Herb promised to give two Saturday mornings a month to occasional maintenance jobs. Martha enrolled in a French class at the University that met two afternoons a week, and joined the Y for a weekly swim class. She elected to keep her job, but henceforth earmarked one-third of her take-home pay exclusively for her own use.

The housework arrangement broke down a few times, but Martha was able to stick to her guns, so that when someone failed to do his job, Martha omitted a chore of hers that affected him. When Herb or one of the boys tried to intimidate her ("Where are my pants?" "Why don't I have any clean socks?"), she would reply, "You didn't do your job, and I assumed that you would rather have me not do mine than walk around feeling victimized and angry with you." As they learned that she meant what she said, she began to enjoy a growing, if occasionally grudging, respect for herself as a person.

Almost immediately after she began to take action on her problem, Martha's depression lifted. She learned that there really were things she could do about her life. She found that she had choices. She discovered that her prison cell had walls of her own making, and that she could step out of the cell and once again assert her rights to be.

If your big question is, "How can I exercise control over my life and still be in contact with others?" learning self-assertion is the answer. A shy person can achieve a certain kind of control by being lonely or withdrawn; or he can achieve a certain kind of contact by giving up control and acting contrary to his own wishes. But if you want both control of your life and contact with others at the same time, you must learn to stand up for yourself, claiming equality with the rest of mankind. In the next chapter we will explore the methods of assertiveness more fully.

# TEN

# Assertiveness Techniques

YOUR HABIT of harshly judging yourself has resulted in the past in your denying yourself the right to be who you are. You have, on the basis of your negative self-concept, consistently put yourself down in comparison to others. We have already examined how harmful—and false—such a negative set of ideas can be. Now we must concentrate on replacing negative ideas with positive ones.

Positive self-valuation means loving yourself. It means recognizing that you are a person of worth and value. It does not mean that you feel superior to all others (if you did you might have other problems). It does mean that you concede to yourself the primary importance of your own happiness and your own self-esteem.

Many shy persons with whom I've worked have reacted with distaste to the idea of positive self-valuation. They have felt that to place a higher value on one's own happiness than on anything else in life is selfish, ungracious, arrogant, obnoxious, and even antireligious. The fact of the matter is that the only way to be

**141**

genuinely useful, good, and desirable to other people is first to be useful, good, and desirable to yourself. Which physician do you want to treat you—the one who entered medicine because he felt it was his duty to humanity, or the one who practices because medicine is what he wants to do more than anything else in life? Would you rather be visited by the neighbor who feels it is his or her obligation to "check in" once a month, or by a friend who comes over because he or she finds pleasure in your company? Are the best letters you write the ones you owe to others, or are they the ones that flow from a sincere desire to make contact? Jesus clearly understood this principle when he instructed his followers to "love thy neighbor *as thyself.*" It is a psychological law that our ability to love others is limited only by the extent to which we love ourselves.

I encourage each of my clients who is in the process of learning assertive behavior to formulate his or her own "emancipation proclamation" in the form of an easily remembered slogan or motto. The basic model I propose is:

> *I have an absolute right to be who I am—to think what I think, feel what I feel, and want what I want.*

Each person may modify the slogan to suit his or her particular tastes and situation but may not weaken, dilute, or qualify the strong statement of his or her right to be.

The advantage of using such a slogan is that little by little it is absorbed into your system of subjective truths, displacing and counteracting the negative effects of your old feeling that other people have a better right to be than you. Some of my clients have printed their slogan on a card and taped it someplace where they will be sure to see it often—over the sink, on the bathroom mirror, on the refrigerator door (where it's particularly helpful for overweight folks who have decided that they have the right to become trim), or on the dashboard of the car. In any case, I recommend at least one slow, deliberate, and thoughtful repetition of the slogan each day during the process of becoming assertive.

Like "shyness," the terms "assertive" and "nonassertive" are not descriptions of people, but of behavior. Although we use the idea of an assertive person as a kind of shorthand, there is really no such thing. There is only assertive (and nonassertive) behavior. The process of becoming assertive, therefore, is a process of changing behavior. Developing a positive self-image and deciding to emancipate oneself will create a mental climate in which assertiveness is logical and appropriate; but in themselves they will not suddenly *cause* assertiveness in everyday situations. First you must learn to change some habits—to do some things differently from the ways you are used to doing them.

In general, three simple guidelines cover almost every instance where assertive behavior is called for. They are:

1. The best way to get what you want is to ask for it.
2. The best way not to get what you don't want is to say no to it.
3. The best way to stop someone from doing some-

thing you don't want them to do is to tell them
how their actions affect you.

The story of one of my clients provides a good illustration of guideline one.

Charles, an executive in a medium-sized firm, who
was seeing me for quite another purpose, mentioned
one day that he had a scheme to obtain a promotion
to a higher-paying job. The head of his department
was moving to a higher position in the home office.
Charles knew that he had superior qualifications and
more experience than anyone else in the office to fill
the vacancy. In addition, he had recently introduced
a new office procedure that had resulted in a 4 percent increase in his branch's profits. Yet he had
learned that the firm had engaged an executive
search agency to find someone outside to replace his
boss.

Charles's plan was complex. He would sponsor an
office party for the departing chief, would arrange
for the report on his new procedure to arrive on his
boss's desk at a propitious time, and would subtly hint
at his career aspirations during moments of casual
conversation.

I proposed the assertive alternative—to ask for the
job—and Charles agreed to take the risk. Together
we rehearsed the way he would ask for what he
wanted. He made an appointment to see his depart-
mental head that week, and made his request this
way:

"I'd like to be considered to fill your spot, Mr.
Hardesty, after you leave. It may be that the company has already considered and rejected me for rea-

sons of its own, but I wanted to at least cover that base with you. My resumé and work record here speak for themselves. The report on my new method for processing credit applications suggests that I've realized many times my salary for the company. Personally, I feel ready for a career move that involves more responsibility. I wondered if you would consider sponsoring me to the management as a candidate to fill your post."

His boss's reply immediately convinced Charles of the value of the assertive approach. "To tell the truth, Charles," he said with a sheepish look, "I've been so preoccupied with my own move that I haven't thought much about my replacement. Naturally the home office wouldn't know your ability as I do, and probably your new procedure shows up on their records as my contribution. Of course I'll recommend you for the job, and thanks for speaking to me about it—I might not even have thought about it otherwise." Charles got the job—and an important insight into how to get what he wanted.

Another of my clients, whose problem doesn't seem to be one of shyness on first glance, had occasion to prove the value of guideline two:

Sally, an attractive, single, twenty-three-year-old secretary, found herself having sex with more people and more often than she wished. On dates she was often filled with anxiety as she tried, usually unsuccessfully, to avoid the question to which she couldn't say no. She usually tried to offer a variety of excuses ("I've got my period," "I live with a roommate," "I have to get up very early") which at best only delayed the inevitable. In therapy, she saw very quickly that her inability to say no was based on a subconscious assumption that the aggressive, economically successful men she usually dated had a better right to sexual pleasure than she had a right to say no, and also on a negative self-concept that led her to believe that the only thing she had to attract men was her sexual favors. The motto she adopted had exclusively to do with sex—"I have an absolute right to be who I want sexually—to enforce my own wishes, to feel attracted to whom I feel attracted, to sleep or not sleep with whomever I want, and only when I want to." Together we practiced a variety of assertive responses stemming from guideline two to fit the various situations in which she found herself.

*For "absolutely not" situations:* "Thank you for the compliment, but I'm really not interested. I think you're a really nice person, but I just don't feel attracted that way. I know you'd rather hear the truth about that than some dishonest excuse."

*For "maybe when I know you better" situations:* "Thank you for the compliment, but for me sex is a very special way of relating that only fits when it's between two people who know each other well and care about each other as people. I think you're really nice, and I'd like to see you again, but I don't feel like we're at a place where sex fits into the picture for me yet."

*For "persistent and repeated requests":* "I want you to know that when you keep asking after I've said no not once but several times, I take it to mean that you don't much care how I feel or what I want. I find that quite annoying and insulting. If that's the case, I guess I don't have the time or energy to spend with people who don't really care about me."

Six months later Sally was living with a man who had come from the "maybe when I know you better" group. He told her later that one of the powerful attractions he felt toward her was that he respected her. "I'm not hung up with a bunch of ideas about not respecting a girl who's 'easy' or 'fast,' " he said, "but I do respect a woman who can't be pushed around, who knows what she wants and doesn't want, and is willing to say so."

The best illustration of the third guideline for assertive behavior is the story of the newlyweds Cynthia and Andy. Andy, you recall, was sexually deflated every time his wife used a certain phrase that she thought was "cute." Andy tried all kinds of indirect, "polite," and nonassertive ways to keep her from using the phrase. He tried kissing her when he thought she was about to say it. He tried to "change the tone" of their relationship by being forceful and dominant. But she didn't get the hard-to-read message and finally he turned off altogether. The irony is that all of their difficulty could have been prevented by a simple assertive statement of the kind indicated by guideline three: "Cynthia, I know you mean well with your 'mama' phrase, and I suppose that to most men it would be cute. But I don't like my mother much, and when you say that, I don't much like the creepy feeling it gives me. I guess I find it a kind of turn-off."

As a special type of self-disclosure, assertive behavior follows all of the rules of self-disclosure that we have discussed earlier:

1. Don't avoid expressing "negative" feelings. They are not "bad" or improper feelings to have.

2. Use "I language" liberally to signify that the statement you are making is an indication of your own feelings. Don't use the pronoun trick.

3. Use "feeling talk" to explain what you feel. *Your* feelings are *your* feelings. You don't have to justify them or make a legal brief for them by making reference to facts or ideas or systems of right and wrong. You only need to state them.

Many of the clients I've encouraged to become assertive have been afraid that assertive behavior is somehow the same as hostile, aggressive behavior. The fear is understandable, but it is not justified. Assertive behavior is standing up for your right to be who you are; aggressive behavior is imposing your will on another person in a way that denies his or her right to be. Assertive behavior discloses your wants, needs, preferences, and plans; aggressive behavior discounts, ignores, or overrides the wants, needs, preferences, and plans of the other person. Assertive behavior acknowledges one's own personhood; aggressive behavior demeans, discounts, or ignores the personhood of the other. Here are some examples of the differences between nonassertive, aggressive, and assertive behaviors:

John and Mary have been dating for two years now. Though they share many interests and get on well in most ways, they have found that they have some significant differences in personal taste. One Friday night John suggests that they take in a rock concert. Mary knows from previous experience that she finds rock concerts unpleasant and nerve-racking. She replies:

NONASSERTIVE: (sigh) "Okay, if you want to."

AGGRESSIVE: "Oh God, how can you even think of it? The idea of the crowds and that miserable electronic screeching and thumping and the ridiculous gyrations of the performers makes me sick! I wish you'd get some idea of civilized taste!"

ASSERTIVE: "Thanks, but I really don't think I'd enjoy that. How about a movie or dinner? Or if it's really important for you to go, I could meet you afterward."

Bob did a research paper in his major field. Although he was an undergraduate, he felt that he had discovered a genuinely new approach to the theoretical problem he had tackled. His paper, graded by the professor's teaching assistant, came back marked "C," with the comment, "This does not conform to accepted opinion on the subject." Bob's responses:

NONASSERTIVE: Accepts the grade, but feels angry and treated unfairly. He turns off on the professor and the course.

AGGRESSIVE: Storms into the professor's office, slaps his paper down on the prof's desk, and says, "Here's another example of how the lousy university system screws the individual student! The stupid T.A. didn't even understand my paper, and of course you don't have time to trouble yourself with reading the work of a lowly undergrad, even though we're paying your salary."

ASSERTIVE: Makes an appointment to see the prof and says, "I could be wrong, but I think that the T.A. just didn't catch my drift on this paper. It's my feeling that the paper is better than the grade it got. I'd appreciate it if you'd read it yourself and let me know what you think."

Roberta's mother comes for a visit. Finding her four-year-old grandson playing with the dog on the floor, she seizes a broom, shoos the dog out the door, kicking him on the way, and berates Roberta for not being a better mother by allowing the child to be exposed to the "filth and disease that animal carries." Roberta responds:

NONASSERTIVE: "Oh Mom, it's not that bad, and besides, we don't let Johnny play with Bobo that often."

AGGRESSIVE: "Who do you think you are, walking in here and telling me how to run my own life? You've always tried to run my life for me! Get out— just get out! Between you and Bobo, I choose Bobo!"

ASSERTIVE: "Mother, Johnny is my child. I'll make the decisions about raising him and I'll be responsible for them. If you can't accept them, you don't have to come here, though I'd be sorry if you felt that way. Now let's get Bobo back before he runs off."

Notice that in every case, the nonassertive response is based on the assumption that the other person has the better right to his plans or preferences than the principal character. The aggressive response, on the other hand, suggests that the other person is bad, stupid, and inferior—it implicitly undermines his right to be who he is. The assertive response simply maintains the personal and absolute right "to be who I am—to think what I think, to feel what I feel, to want what I want." The assertive response fulfills the needs and wants of the principal character without sacrificing the personhood of either party.

Being nonassertive, in fact, is far more likely to result eventually in aggressive behavior. When a person consistently denies himself or herself the right to be a person, the inner need to be and the anger at not being will build up tremendous pressure and will finally result in an aggressive and destructive explosion of anger. An overwhelming number of divorces occur when the partner who had passively and even smilingly borne nonpersonhood for years one day blows up or just leaves. Often the assertive partner never understands what happened. In an almost paradoxical way, the more you develop consistently assertive behavior, the more you ensure yourself against developing aggressive behavior. Aggressive behavior is the frightened, defensive retaliation of a person whose right to be is threatened. Appropriately assertive behavior ensures that your right to be who you are is never threatened to the degree that you need to lash out.

While assertiveness is not hostile or aggressive, by the same token it won't make everything happen just the way you want it to. Practicing assertiveness will give you more control of your life and improve the chances of your getting what you want, of avoiding what you don't want, and of deepening your relationships with others. But it can only increase your control over your own life; it can't give you control over the lives and behavior of others. From your own experience you know the unhappiness of placing the wants and needs of others before your own. So it would be a mistake to expect others to place your needs and wants before their own.

Part of the process of making genuine contact involves acknowledging that another person's wants and needs will not always coincide with your own. Perhaps this is the meaning of the late Fritz Perls's famous little saying:

> You do your thing, and I'll do mine.
> I am not in this world to fill your expectations,
> and you are not in this world to fill mine.
> If by chance we meet, it's beautiful.
> If not, it can't be helped.

Suppose that you and another person "don't meet," that is, your needs and wants contradict each other in a way that appears to be mutually exclusive. What then? Your way of resolving this problem in the past, of course, has been to be nonassertive, to place the other's wants and needs before your own. The result has been anger, depression and, ultimately, loss of contact. There are, however, at least three ways in which you can resolve a situation of this kind without denial of your right to be, and without loss of contact. They are compromise, deliberate deferral of one's needs in preference to the other, and agreed-upon independent pursuit of both agendas.

Compromise is a tricky and often unsatisfying method for resolving conflicting needs. Folk wisdom, with a fair degree of accuracy, defines compromise as a situation in which "one person wants to do one thing, another person wants to do something else, and both end up doing something neither wants to do."

Compromise does work occasionally, however. In

order for it to be successful, at least two moderately unusual conditions must exist:

1. Both parties must agree on the ultimate goal of the relationship or plan.

2. Both must be quite open about their preferences and assertive in the process of negotiating (clearly stating what they are willing to concede and what they are not).

If one or both of these conditions is lacking, compromise turns into struggle, one person inevitably ends up giving up a part of his or her right to be, and the quality of contact suffers.

A second way to resolve conflicting needs and wants is by deliberate deferring the needs of one in favor of the needs of the other. This is less tricky to achieve, but far more prone to lead to a pattern of nonassertiveness on the part of one partner.

> Jake was exhausted when he arrived home after a two-week business trip that had been nearly nonstop meetings on a project of great importance to his company. An hour after he arrived home, his wife, Doris, received a call from her mother informing her that her father, whom Jake had only met twice, had been diagnosed as having a terminal cancer and was not expected to live more than six months. Doris was understandably shaken, and only an hour after Jake had collapsed into bed for his long-anticipated sleep, Doris shook him gently and said, "Jake, I'm so upset I can't sleep. I really need to talk." Jake decided deliberately to set aside his need for sleep in favor of Doris's need to talk about her father.

In order for deliberate deferral of one partner's needs not to lead to a pattern of nonassertiveness and noncontact, the situation must be very clearly understood by both partners:

1. The partner who decides to defer his own needs is doing so out of choice, not because he must.

2. The needs he defers are clearly stated, and no attempt to minimize their importance is made. (It would have been a noncontactful lie if Jake had said, "Sure, Honey, I don't feel much like sleeping anyway.")

3. Both parties realize that one partner, in setting aside his needs, has created a deficit in his own happiness that must eventually balance out if the relationship is to continue successfully.

4. Deferral of needs must not consistently run in one direction only. Constant surrender of one person's rights to happiness in favor of another's is the definition of nonassertiveness. Frustration, anger, depression, and noncontact are the inevitable results.

Often, the best alternative for resolving conflicting needs is the mutually respectful agreement of both parties to pursue their needs independently. At first glance this alternative would appear to destroy contact rather than help it. When we look closer, however, we see that when needs conflict in such a way as to be genuinely contradictory over a significant period of time, being together can only mean that one person gives up his right to what he needs and wants. If both parties agree to follow their needs independently, they are fully recognizing each other's right to be.

Ari and Laurel were two young people who had fallen deeply in love. By all external criteria they were the perfect match. Both were professionals who, in their middle twenties, had already achieved significant successes in their shared field. Both had an almost fanatic interest in horses, which they shared with each other in a way they couldn't with their less-involved friends. They enjoyed hiking and skiing together. They both had a "shameful" capacity for self-indulgence, were able to enjoy good food, good liquor, good music, good sex, and leisure to the very limits of their resources.

After two years together, however, it became clear that they differed at the level of some very deeply felt needs and wants. Ari, the product of a severely disrupted home as a child, and on his own since age fifteen, wanted to settle into a long-term relationship with the woman he loved, to make a home together, and rely on the security of this primary relationship. Laurel, whose childhood had been far more stable and whose young adulthood was more conventional, felt an overpowering need to explore herself as a person, to grow, to answer questions about who she really was. Could she make it in life on her own? How would she relate to other kinds of men?

As each felt the undeniable press of their conflicting needs, they tried to sit on them, in the interests of preserving their "ideal" relationship. She tried valiantly to become more domestic, more demonstratively loving. He alternately struggled to understand and ignored her longing glances at other men. In doing so, both were denying their own rights to be who they were, and their contact decreased until it seemed that the only contact they had was in their arguments.

It was Laurel who, though outwardly more uncertain, was really the one more willing to face facts and deal with life as it was. She finally made them both deal with the "If not, it can't be helped" part of Perls's saying. She moved out of the house that they shared, and set about answering her questions about life. After a period in which Ari continued to deny reality and tried to draw her back into the old relationship, they agreed that it was too painful for them to continue to see one another. They agreed she would continue to seek answers to her questions, and he would remain open to establishing the kind of relationship he wanted with another partner. Their parting was sad and painful, but it was based on true contact, a recognition of and a respect for the personhood of the other.

These two chapters on assertiveness are not intended to be a comprehensive program. Several fine books are available that can help you develop assertive behavior and learn more about it. Among them are Dr. Herbert Fensterheim's *Don't Say Yes When You Want To Say No* (New York: David McKay Co., Inc., 1975), Manuel J. Smith's *When I Say No I Feel Guilty* (New York: Dial Press, 1975), and *The Assertive Woman* by Lynn Bloom and Karen Coburn (New York: Delacorte Press, 1975).

As your skills at assertiveness grow, you will find that the quality of your contact with others will improve significantly. As you experience your right to be, the person you really are will "come out of the closet." The people you have contact with will know you in a deeper and clearer way.

# ELEVEN

# Making Contact at Work

MOST SHY PEOPLE I've worked with have been particularly concerned with overcoming their shyness in one of the specific areas discussed in the following chapters: at work, in romantic and sexual situations, and in long-term relationships such as marriage. The final chapter, on making contact in a social situation, serves as a review of the rest of the book, describing the techniques we have discussed as they appear in action.

The following suggestions for applying your new contact skills can only be guidelines, not sure-fire formulas. Contact is an evolving process between two people and each occurrence is unique. Relationships grow and prosper or sicken and die just like living things. The techniques we have described can create a promising climate for satisfying relationships, but they can't guarantee the relationships themselves. As you become more at home with feeling in contact with others, you will gradually free yourself of the rules and admonitions in this book, feeling it appropriate to use some of the techniques, and to ignore or perhaps deliberately violate some others. Perhaps the only fixed rule in making contact is to be as open to your own experience and as responsive to the other person's experience as possible.

Most of us spend eight hours or more of each weekday at work. Very few of us would say we were there principally to enjoy contact with others. Yet the chance to work with congenial people can make an otherwise unremarkable job a pleasure. Indeed, for just this reason, some of us choose types of work in which the pay and other conditions are less than the best.

Shy people as a group miss out on a great deal of satisfaction at work because they find it so difficult to make any meaningful contact with their fellow workers. They do their jobs in isolated silence, speaking only when spoken to. They tend to sit apart on lunch hours and coffee breaks. To their fellow workers they are mystery people whose silence and nonverbal signals discourage approach. They don't get invited to parties or stop off with colleagues for coffee or cocktails after work. They may fail to get promotions because they are unknown quantities to their superiors. And employers often take advantage of them because they are not assertive enough to say no to longer hours or to tasks that should not be part of their responsibilities. Rather than making work an important way of extending themselves outward into the world, shy people treat a job simply as a courtyard to their personal prison, a place where they take their exercise each day.

Of course work offers some obstacles to contact. Most jobs are primarily solitary. Sitting at a typewriter, operating a machine, doing paper work are activities that are done alone. In some situations time is so rigidly structured that there are few opportunities for personal contact during working hours. In fact, some employers intentionally reduce contact between employees, believing it will decrease their production. Competitive feelings in various jobs may cause some workers to not be friendly with others.

Still, work has many built-in advantages for establishing contact. Jobs bring people together in the same time and place over a long period of time. Employees often feel drawn together by common experiences and emotions—whether by enthusiams for the task at hand or by dislike of a boss. In some ways the job provides especially promising chances for the shy person to find friends. Work situations are less fluid than most social situations—everyone has his or her place, the job provides a common topic of conversation, and people are not usually judged on the fine points of their appearance and social graces. Most jobs contain some structured lunch or break times during which socializing is easy and natural. Additionally, a person who still lacks self-confidence can make casual friends on the job without the pressure to "get serious" that is often felt in dating and party situations.

## Identifying Shyness in Work Situations

Most job situations offer some convenient checkpoints at which you can observe your own shyness. Behavior patterns become clear very quickly because the daily routine provides a perfect backdrop against which to observe them. Here are a few of the most obvious checkpoints for you to work with. If you can think of others that fit your particular job, add them.

1. arrival at work
2. coffee break
3. lunch hour
4. working on something with others
5. business meetings
6. contact with the public

If you will take time to describe yourself in detail in each of these situations, you will see which ones cause you to act shy and withdrawn. Here are some typical behavioral descriptions of shy people in work situations:

1. *Arrival at work*—"I drive alone to work, planning so as to arrive about half an hour early. I stop at the coffee shop across the street, and have coffee and read the paper. Then I go to the office. (If there are people I know waiting at the elevator, I hang back so I don't have to ride with them.) When I enter the office, I go straight to my desk. It seems to me I look mostly at the floor or straight ahead of me. If someone else says, 'Good morning,' then I do, but otherwise I don't speak to anyone, or I simply nod."

2. *Coffee break*—"Usually I stay at my desk and read a book or work on a letter to someone."

3. *Lunch break*—"Since I bring my lunch, it's usually the same story as coffee break. When the weather is really nice, I'll go to the park. Sometimes a group goes to lunch, and asks me along. That's hard—I kind of want to go, but I feel afraid somehow, so I always say no."

4. *Working on something with others*—"These are very uncomfortable situations for me. It always seems that the other people are better at the job than I am.

I wait until someone seems to be running the show and then take my directions from that person. Sometimes I feel I've got a better idea about how to get things done, but I never say so, because it doesn't seem worth the embarrassment and hassle."

5. *Business meetings*—"I observe the old saying they used to tell the soldiers in the trenches: 'Keep your head down and you won't get it blown off.' I plan my arrival to be at the tail end of on-time—that way I don't have to make conversation with the early-comers and at the same time I don't attract attention by being late. While waiting to get started I pretend to study my materials. I don't volunteer comments, nor do I ask questions (I always think I'll look stupid or incompetent). Before every meeting I try to rehearse the answers to any questions I might be asked, but I'm still afraid I won't be able to answer."

6. *Contact with the public*—"This is a bit easier, because I know I'll probably never see them again. Basically, I let them talk to me. They say what they want, I try to take care of it. Sometimes they just want to chat, but I don't know what to say, so I just stick to the job."

It makes sense that your first step toward changing shy behavior should be to change the kind of negative thinking that leads to the behavior (see Chapter 4 for directions). The idea is to define who you want to be at work, and then to use your imagination to think your way into a new set of subjective truths.

Once you've begun to change your negative subjective truths into more positive ones, you must specify the exact behavioral changes you need to make in order to stop being shy. Go back over your descriptions of your behavior at each of the work-situation checkpoints. If you've put enough energy into the descriptions, you should be able to spot a number of behaviors you want to change. On a separate sheet of paper, list on the left-hand side of the page all of the problem behaviors you can spot. On the right side, list alternatives that would promote better contact. The completed sheet might look like the one on the facing page.

Once you've pinpointed the behaviors that make you shy at work and imagined some alternatives, you can put into action the following four-point program:

1. Write or record a description of yourself performing each of the alternative behaviors, whether you actually intend to use them or not.

2. List the alternative behaviors in order of their difficulty for you, from the easiest to the hardest.

3. Using a cassette recorder, describe yourself performing each new behavior, one at a time, from the easiest to the hardest.

4. After one week of practice in your imagination, make it your goal to perform alternative behavior number one (the easiest in real life). After you have done it five or six times, it will become a learned skill that will be available to you whenever you want it. Then move on to behavior number two, and so on.

Within an amazingly short period of time you will find that you have replaced the behaviors that made you shy at work with a new set of behaviors that tend to increase the possibility of contact. Don't be discouraged if it takes your fellow workers awhile to react to the changes you're making. After all, for as long as

|  | **Problem Behavior** | **Alternative** |
|---|---|---|
| 1. Arrival at work | 1. drive alone<br>2. coffee shop<br>3. elevator<br>4. walk to desk | 1. bus? car pool?<br>2. bring coffee, drink it in the office and chat<br>3. try to ride elevator with fellow workers<br>4. smile, make eye contact, say "good morning" to others |
| 2. Coffee break | 1. sit at desk | 1. sit with others |
| 3. Lunch hour | 1. sit at desk and eat from brown bag<br>2. go for walk<br>3. decline invitation | 1. sit with others and eat from brown bag<br><br>2. invite someone to go for walk<br>3. (a) accept invitation<br>   (b) invite someone |
| 4. Cooperative project | 1. wait for directions<br>2. keep quiet | 1. take initiative<br>2. propose ideas |
| 5. Business meetings | 1. time arrival<br><br>2. pretend to study materials<br>3. don't volunteer comment<br>4. don't ask questions | 1. (a) arrive early (preferably)<br>   (b) arrive late<br>2. chat with others<br>3. volunteer comment<br>4. ask questions |
| 6. Contact with public | 1. wait for them to talk to me<br>2. stick to business when they want to chat | 1. smile, make eye contact, ask how to be of help<br>2. use active listening when they have something to say |

you've worked with them they've seen you as a withdrawn, isolated loner. You trained them to see you that
way by discouraging their friendly overtures. It's up to
you to retrain them to see you as someone they can
have contact with. Stick with it, and in a short time
you'll discover that there are people at work whose
experiences you can share and who want to share yours.

## Making Conversation at Work

Establishing contact with others at work through conversation follows all of the conversation patterns in any
other setting, subject only to a few modifications im-
posed by the structure of the work itself.

One of the best patterns of effective listening is the
combination of ritual questions, information-seeking
questions, and active listening. (For a review of these
techniques, see Chapter 5.)

Ritual questions are like a verbal handshake. It makes
sense, then, that your first ritual question of the day
should be coupled with your first greeting. Shy people
are often chronic nongreeters. Begin to train yourself
to say "Hi," or "Good morning," to each person you
meet. Then ask, "How are you?" Everyone recognizes
that this question is not really a request for information
(as it would be if a doctor were asking it of a patient in
the hospital, for example). Consider the following ex-
change: "How are you?" With a smile, "Terrible." With
a bigger smile, "That's good." The trick is to ask in such
a way that you assure the other person of your goodwill.
Practice using ritual questions and greetings in front of
a mirror, imagining each of your co-workers in turn.

One of the differences between contact at work and contact in social situations is that contact at work is often interrupted by the demands of the job. Needless to say, you don't give a new greeting or ritual question at each coffee break or lull in the work schedule. In work situations the information-seeking question becomes a kind of ritual question to reopen the communication that was previously interrupted.

John comes to work one morning. On the way to his desk, he stops at Bill's desk and says, "Hi, Bill, how are you today?" "Hassled," says Bill. "The dog got sick last night and we had to take him to the vet, I put a dent in my car on the way to work, and . . . " He is about to go on when his phone rings. John goes to his desk. A little later, at the coffee break, John sits down with Bill and says, "So what's wrong with the dog?" John has overcome the interruption by continuing the conversation at the next appropriate time.

Since you encounter people at work regularly over a period of months or years, you often have a chance to continue conversation on a topic over a long period. For example, John knows that Bill was making plans last spring to build a boat in his backyard this summer. Weeks later, he asks, "How's the boat coming?"

At the beginning of an acquaintance, however, you must ask questions for which there is no previous background. For example:

> "What part of town do you live in?"
> "Where are you going on your vacation?"
> "I'm looking for a good hair stylist (or insurance

agent or automobile mechanic). Can you recommend one?"

"How is your family?"

Keep in mind that taking the initiative is your responsibility. Chances are that you trained people you work with not to make contact with you (whether you realized you were doing it or not). When they approached you in the past, you put on a deadpan expression, looked away, closed your posture, leaned or faced away, and gave short, uninviting answers. The message was that you didn't want contact. So now it's up to you to make it clear that you've changed.

As soon as ritual questions and greetings become comfortable for you, make a list of appropriate information-seeking questions to ask your co-workers. What do you know about them? Does Charley have a family? Is Annette working on a special project? Did Arlo just buy a vacation cabin? People love to talk about what interests them, and you can use their interests as points for first contact.

When you draw a substantial response to a ritual or information-seeking question, remember the technique of active listening. Active listening conveys to people that what they are telling you is important and interesting to you and gives them the freedom to share without fear of judgment, ridicule, interruption, or rejection. Notice how John uses active listening when Bill responds to a question about progress on building his boat:

JOHN: "How's the boat coming?"

BILL: "Well, I still want to build it really bad, but

I had no idea how much was involved."

JOHN: "Hm. It must be that when you get down to what's actually involved, it gets pretty complicated."

BILL: "Oh yeah. Gee, even deciding what plan to use is a major problem all by itself!"

JOHN: "There must be several designs to choose from, then."

BILL: "You bet. In the 32-foot class, which is the general size I'm planning on, there are sloop designs, ketch designs, single-mast designs, and there's something to be said for each of 'em."

At the end of the conversation, Bill feels that John was really interested in him and his project. John is pleased that Bill shared that part of his experience with him. Assuming that Bill eventually moves beyond sailboats to sharing other parts of his experience and shows some interest in finding out about John and his life, this could be the beginning of a warm friendship.

## Sending Nonverbal Signals at Work

The role that nonverbal signals play in promoting or discouraging contact cannot be overemphasized. As I pointed out in Chapter 6, the shy person consistently transmits signals that say, "Don't approach! Go away! Don't talk to me!" If you want to make contact, you must take the responsibility of beginning to transmit the nonverbal signals that invite rather than turn away. Review the SOFTEN behaviors described in Chapter 6: Smile, Open posture, Forward lean, Touch, Eye contact, and Nod. These signals together will say, "I am interested in you. Please approach me."

If you doubt the importance of the nonverbal signals, try this simple experiment. Pick out the person at your place of work who is the most shy and the person who is the least shy. Watch the two of them over a period of several days and compare them on the SOFTEN behaviors. You needn't even talk to the two people yourself since these behaviors can be observed all the way across a room. Invariably you will find that the nonshy person uses all or nearly all of the SOFTEN behaviors regularly (even though he or she has probably never heard of them!). The shy person rarely uses any of the behaviors, and the message of the opposite signals is very clear—without a word being spoken. This experiment should encourage you to brush up on the SOFTEN behaviors yourself. Practice them in front of a mirror and when you feel you have command of them, make it your goal to use them all at least once when talking to another person. Once you succeed, try using them twice, then three times. In a short time the positive nonverbal signals will be part of your natural behavior and you will do them without having to think.

## *Turning Contact into Friendship*

Developing friendships with work associates is a very natural process, demanding only your willingness to step out of your self-made prison cell and to reach out toward others. Friendships develop wherever contact occurs, and since you probably spend more of your waking hours at your place of work than at any other place, a greater likelihood exists that you will find friendships there.

In order for a friendship to develop from a work association, three steps must be completed:

Step 1. The two (or more) people must experience some contact in the work situation itself, and feel positive about it.

Step 2. The two must experience some contact in a social setting directly connected with the work situation (e.g., coffee break, lunch, coffee or drinks after work), and feel positive about it.

Step 3. The two must experience some contact away from the work setting, arranged purely to spend time together, and both must feel positive about it.

Here are some examples of how this process might work:

> Alice and Joanne are secretaries in the same office of a downtown law firm. Over the five months since Alice joined the office staff, she and Joanne have had a number of pleasant conversations during lulls in the work day (Step 1). Last week, on Joanne's birthday, they went out to lunch at a nearby restaurant, and Alice bought Joanne a birthday drink (Step 2). On Friday afternoon, in response to Joanne's question about what she had planned for the weekend, Alice said, "Well, that new Italian movie, *Red Sunset Over the Mediterranean* is playing at the Tivoli . . . but I'm afraid no date came through for tonight." Joanne replied, "Me either—hey, why don't we have dinner after work and go to the movies together?" (Step 3).

Carl and Vaughn knew each other slightly from the office, but had never said more than hello to one another until they were selected to represent their two departments at a regional conference in Los Angeles. They sat together on the plane and found they had a good deal in common, including the fact that their wives had both come from the same small town in the eastern part of the state (Step 1). After the first day's business meetings, they went to a boat show together, because Vaughn had a boat and Carl was considering buying one (Step 2). On the way back home, Vaughn suggested that the two couples get together for a day of sailing a week from the following Sunday (Step 3).

Steve and Joline were in the same sociology class. They were teamed by the professor to work on a presentation for class (Step 1). Part of the task involved seeing a correctional facility some forty miles from the University. In the car going to and from the prison, they talked a good deal about each other's future plans (Step 2). A week after their presentation, Steve called and asked Joline to go dancing (Step 3).

How can you begin to turn some of your work contacts into genuine friendships? The key is to get yourself into the process. You don't have to worry about the goal. If you will engage in the process as in Step 1, by using your new nonshy skills, sooner or later it will become very natural for you to move into Step 2 by asking or being asked to go on a coffee break or lunch with someone else. If you feel good about that contact, then Step 3 is a logical evolution. The only part of the process toward which you need direct any deliberate, intentional action is Step 1. The way to do this, as we have discussed, is to identify the problem behaviors that have contributed to your shyness, and then change them, using the techniques of imagination, verbal communication, and nonverbal signaling to indicate to others that you are really interested in them and in the contact they can provide.

# TWELVE

# Making Sexual Contact

MAKING SEXUAL CONTACT is not simply the process of getting someone to go to bed with you. It is far more complex than that, and it includes a period of often delicate preliminaries known as "dating," or "courtship," or just "getting acquainted." Everyone has sexual needs, but in my experience trying to have sex with someone with whom you have made no other real kind of contact is both difficult and (when it does come about) ultimately unsatisfying.

Sex that is satisfying and not destructive is closely related to our need for closeness with another person. Contactful sex is a very powerful way of learning and sharing with another what it means to be human.

Shy people have some special problems in dating, courtship, and sexual situations. They are naturally reluctant to open themselves to an intense relationship because they fear they may reveal their differentness and inferiority. They are unskilled in or totally ignorant of the verbal and nonverbal signals that lead to sexual closeness, and they often feel ashamed of their own

**173**

sexual desires. For all these reasons, the shy person seldom allows a situation to develop that may lead to sexual contact.

Here are some typical stories of how shy people fail to make sexual contact:

> Elton is a twenty-nine-year-old biologist. Although he has had two long-term relationships with women and several casual sexual encounters, he is not sure how those experiences developed. For a long time his method of trying to promote sexual contact was to frequent singles bars and "present" himself to women who seemed to be available. He introduced himself, rather frantically told about his work, his income, his handsome bachelor apartment. This may seem like nonshy behavior, but Elton was using bluster to cover up his feelings of inferiority. He hoped the women would be "snowed" by his act and would elect to spend the night with him. The problem was that he invariably "struck out."
>
> Elton concluded that he was "not good enough" to attract a woman with honest bluster, so he began to lie. He introduced himself as a physician, quoted his salary at three or four times its true level. He went on crash diets and spent far more than he could afford on inappropriately impressive clothes. His reasoning was that he could straighten out the lies after a relationship got under way. But he continued to fail to make even casual sexual contact. No doubt the women he met saw through his come-on and read another signal that he was sending unconsciously:

"I'm not who you think I am and I'm scared to death."

Marty is a twenty-seven-year-old nurse. Coming from a rigidly moralistic Roman Catholic childhood in a small rural community, she had (with some embarrassment) reached the age of twenty-seven still a virgin. Of even more concern, however, there seemed to be little chance that the situation would change. She lived alone. The few friendships she had were with other nurses, and the only men she knew were her girlfriends' husbands or boyfriends.

Occasionally Marty would be asked for a date, sometimes by men she worked with, but more often by men her friends had "set her up" with. Sometimes when she was invited out, she would feel a sense of panic and would make up some excuse to turn the invitation down.

When she did accept a date, things didn't go well. She had difficulty talking to a man. She did the opposite of all the SOFTEN behaviors. She felt awkward and unattractive. She would start to tell her date something about herself, then stop because it seemed so trivial and unimportant. And running through her mind the whole evening was anxiety about "what might happen later." On the few occasions when her dates were not frightened off by her behavior and did try to hold her hand or kiss her, she would get almost panicky and would put a stop to physical contact before it began.

Neither of these persons seemed to understand that sexual contact is a special form of the same process we have been describing as "contact." When two people feel both an emotional and a physical attraction to each other, their contact often leads sooner or later to sex. But making genuine interpersonal contact is a prerequisite to making satisfying sexual contact. Since this is the case, let's review what is necessary:

1. Identifying and giving up your negative and unhelpful ideas about yourself. In a sexual contact situation, ideas of inferiority often appear as negative feelings about one's own attractiveness or as feelings that sex is nasty, dirty, or sinful.

2. Giving the other person assurance of his or her own importance as a human being. In making sexual contact, you do this as in any other kind of contact. Use questioning and active listening, and in general show you're interested in your friend's total experience.

3. Using nonverbal signals to emphasize your verbal interest in the other person. In making sexual contact, the two most important of the SOFTEN behaviors are the forward lean (which says, "I want to be physically close to you") and touch (which says, "I get pleasure from the feel of your body").

4. Disclosing your thoughts, feelings, and experiences to others. In making sexual contact, this should include simple but direct statements of your feelings toward the other person, such as, "I'm feeling very attracted to you."

5. Maintaining your right to be by being appropriately assertive. Assertiveness applies to sexual contact primarily when you wish to make a verbal sexual proposition, or at times when you wish to say no to someone else's proposition.

## *Making the Most of What You Have*

Our culture has evolved an unholy worship of youth, slimness, and beauty that makes all but the most perfectly endowed of us feel vaguely ashamed of our bodies. Advertisers' images of what we should look and be like are so powerful that few of us, if any, are wholly unaffected by them.

Your ability to find and make sexual contact is primarily a matter of your capacity to make *interpersonal* contact. Physical attractiveness is only a secondary consideration. There are many exceedingly attractive people who are virtually unable to make interpersonal contact and thus fail to make sexual contact as well. On the other hand, even Phyllis Diller, our country's most celebrated "antibeauty" queen, had her husband "Fang," who, though the butt of many of her jokes, is also obviously the object of much of her affection.

Although physical attractiveness is only a secondary factor in sexual contact, the fact remains that it is a factor. Sex is partly a matter of aesthetics. I believe, however, that once you've mastered the interpersonal skills, the real issue becomes not finding things to increase your physical attractiveness, but learning to avoid those things that decrease it.

So the real question is, "Are you making the most of what you have?" You don't need more cosmetics, a better cologne, padded bras, or more expensive suits to make you more of a turn-on. You do need to be sure that you aren't, through ignorance or neglect, making yourself a *turn-off*. You don't need to make yourself something you're not in order to enjoy sexual contact, but you do need to make the best of what you are.

Make yourself a checklist of the physical features you present to others, and consider each in terms of whether it's as attractive as you can make it:

|        |          |
|--------|----------|
| hair   | odor     |
| teeth  | weight   |
| skin   | clothing |

Taking good care of your appearance should grow to be a natural activity—not just to impress others but because you care about yourself and feel that the attractive well-cared-for you is the "real you." It's amazing how warmly other people respond to you when you feel good about yourself!

## Signaling Sexual Availability

Signaling your availability for sexual contact requires both verbal and nonverbal signals. Verbally you indicate to your prospective partner that there are no obstacles in his or her way. You make it clear that you have no steady partner (for example, by referring to a recent divorce or break-up, by indicating that you live alone, etc.) and that you are not opposed to sexual activity. CAUTION: Don't try to follow these suggestions by making up things that aren't true; part of the point of contact is to be honest.

Nonverbally, you signal your availability for sexual contact by using the SOFTEN behaviors. In the appropriate setting, with a prospective partner who is available and attracted to you, your SOFTEN signs, particularly leaning close and touching, will be seen as messages of sexual availability. By the same token, in situations where you want to discourage sexual contact, the opposite of the SOFTEN behaviors are signals of *non*-availability.

## Minimizing the Risks of Rejection

Most sexually available people, shy and nonshy alike, make far fewer sexual invitations than would be accepted if they made them. The reason this is true is that people fear rejection. When we make a sexual invitation, we place ourselves in a very vulnerable position. We ask implicitly whether the prospective partner likes us well enough and finds us desirable enough to want to have sex with us. If a "no" answer is given, we take it, rightly or wrongly, not as just a no to sex, but also as a no to us as persons. And for the shy or nonshy, that hurts.

Shy people, of course, make even fewer sexual invitations than nonshy people. The more negative subjective truths we hold, the greater the chance of rejection we believe there is. If I believe that I am stupid, or ugly, or otherwise unappealing, then it follows I believe that other people would not accept sexual invitations from me. Therefore, I do not make them. Even after you have let go of those negative ideas about yourself, however, making a sexual invitation is still a risk, a gamble. Although we can minimize the possibility of rejection, we cannot eliminate it.

If you will learn a few simple rules, you can place yourself in a position where, when you make a sexual invitation, you will know in advance that the odds are good that you'll get a yes. Here they are:

1. Don't make a sexual invitation to someone you know is married or has a steady partner. Even if you feel attracted and it seems clear to you that the other person is attracted to you, be content to signal your availability, but leave it to him or her to make the invitation.

2. Wait until you feel that you're really in contact before making an invitation. You don't have a deadline to meet. If you don't feel you've really gotten close to the other person's thoughts, feelings, and experiences, wait until you do. Don't make an invitation for form's sake.

3. Look for signals of availability, both verbal and nonverbal. Listen also for signals from your prospective partner indicating a generally open attitude toward sexual contact. Look for nonverbal messages of the SOFTEN behaviors, especially touching and forward leaning.

4. Notice any signs of physical arousal, but don't wait for them to make your invitation. In men, of course, the most obvious sign of physical arousal is an erection. In women, the erectile tissue of the nipples may become noticeable even under clothing. In both sexes, facial flushing, mild perspiration, and dilated pupils may be signs of physical arousal, but may also come from alcohol or exercise. Many people do not become aroused except when touched in an explicitly sexual way.

5. Know that the probability of a yes to your invitation rises with each successive time you are together— up to a point. Going to bed with someone requires a certain amount of trust, and it takes some folks longer to trust than others. For many people, it's easier to say

yes the second or third or fourth time together than the first, although if everything in numbers 1–4 is happening the first time you're together, there's no ironclad rule against making your invitation. If, however, you wait too long to make your invitation, the other person may conclude that you just aren't interested, and automatically shut down his or her sexual responses to you in order to avoid frustration. The right time to make your invitation is when rules 1–3, and perhaps 4, are clearly in effect.

If you've observed all the above, and are still rejected, you've been "led on." Don't be embarrassed. It was the other person who acted inappropriately by signaling things he or she didn't mean. You responded completely appropriately by making your invitation. Know that in the long run, far, far more of your invitations will be accepted than rejected if you follow these rules.

## How To Make a Sexual Invitation

In 99 percent of initial sexual encounters, the two partners are not spontaneously swept into bed in a sunburst of passion to the accompaniment of violins and flutes. The other one percent mostly occurs in movies. In order for the vast majority of initial sexual encounters to occur at all, *somebody* has to make a direct, verbal invitation. In the interest of being responsible for your own feelings of attraction, and helping what you want to happen, it may as well be you.

The trick to making a proper sexual invitation is to be clear and direct without being clumsy or more explicit than the situation calls for. Being clear means indicating that sex is what you have in mind. Don't say, "I'd like you to come up to my apartment so that we can be together awhile longer." Don't say, "I'd like to see you again because I'm fascinated by your political philosophy" if you mean "I'd like to see you again because I feel really attracted to you."

Being direct means owning up to your own feelings by using "I language" and putting your invitation in the form of a statement. It's you who feels the attraction. It's you who wants to make sexual contact. Don't cop out by putting your invitation in the form of a question which, by answering, makes the other person responsible for your intentions. Don't say, "Would you like to come home with me and spend the night?" Do say, "I'd like it if you would come home with me and spend the night."

Not being clumsy simply means taking a moment to plan the exact wording of your invitation, and making it at the appropriate time. Don't make your invitation in the presence of a third person. Don't make your invitation in the middle of an entirely unrelated conversation. Don't interrupt something your prospective partner is saying to make your invitation (he or she may be working up to one of their own!). Don't make your invitation when your prospective partner is really "into" doing something else, like dancing, partying, being with other friends, etc. The ideal time to make your invitation is when conditions 1–3, and perhaps 4 and 5, are in effect, when what you've both been doing seems to be over or winding down, when the further options seem to be to go home alone or spend more time together, and when a lull in the conversation makes a new subject appropriate.

## Assertiveness and Sexual Contact

Assertiveness, you will remember, is granting yourself the right to be the person you are. Being sexually assertive means recognizing that you are a sexual being with sexual needs and desires and giving yourself the right to try to fulfill those desires when, where, and with whom you choose to.

The three guidelines to assertive behavior are:

1. The best way to get what you want is to ask for it.
2. The best way not to get what you don't want is to say no to it.
3. The best way to influence another person's behavior is to tell him how it makes you feel.

Each of these three guidelines has a special application in making sexual contact. The first guideline suggests that if sexual contact is what you want, the best way to go about getting it is to make sexual invitations. To do so involves overcoming the fear of rejection and the vague sense of shame about your body and your sexual impulses which our culture teaches us from earliest childhood on. The fact is that when you are shy and relatively inexperienced, extending a sexual invitation is scary. It is also true, however, that it becomes easier and smoother and less frightening every time you do it.

If you continue your loneliness and sexual frustration, it only gets more and more painful.

I have tried as conscientiously as possible to make this chapter as nonsexist as possible. I believe that women can and should (and do, more and more) pursue sexual contact as actively as men are traditionally supposed to do. But even I must admit that the second guideline to assertive behavior, as it applies to sex, is more a woman's issue than a man's. As a person whose right it is to fulfill your own sexual needs and wants when, where, and with whom you choose, it is also your absolute right to say no to any sexual invitation that you are inclined not to accept. You are not obligated to give a reason for your nonacceptance, though it is comforting to the other person if there is a reason that has nothing to do with him. (See the case of Sally, pp. 145–147.)

The third guideline to assertive behavior, "The best way to influence someone else's behavior is to tell him how it makes you feel," has more to do with what you do in bed than with what's involved in getting there. The point is that you have a right to sexual gratification (that's why you're involved in making sexual contact, isn't it?) and telling your partner how to please you is the best way to obtain that gratification.

## Where Can You Make Sexual Contact?

The simplest answer to this question is, "Anywhere there's an available member of the sex of your preference." People want to make contact. If I've made nothing else clear in this book, let that be clear. The world is full of all kinds of people who want to make all kinds of contact, and that includes sexual contact. They're at work, at classes, at school, in the next apartment, at the laundromat, at parties, at restaurants and cocktail lounges.

A word about "singles bars." Singles bars operate on the seduction model, not on the contact principle. The general level of anxiety in a typical singles bar is high to the point of painful; success is measured by "scoring," not contact. Nonetheless, singles bars do provide a kind of low-quality, high-volume sexual outlet for some people. If you're a proverbial Venus or Adonis with a line of chatter equaled only by your local used-car dealer, you might want to give one a try. Otherwise, my advice would be to steer clear.

There are, however, places where the probability of making contact with someone who's sexually available is higher than in your empty living room. Here are some suggestions:

1. *Parties*—let your close friends know that you're interested in meeting more people, and ask to be invited to their parties (they may have been assuming that because of your shyness you'd rather not go). Consider giving a party yourself.

2. *Noncredit classes*—many colleges and high schools conduct an amazing variety of skills and hobbies courses. Chances are that if you're interested in guitar playing, or hand-loom weaving, or whatever, you immediately have a point of contact with some available person in the class.

3. *Church social groups*—many churches sponsor groups whose membership is not limited to church members.

4. *Community or charity projects*—volunteers are always needed.

5. *Special interest groups*—dogs, motorcycle touring, sixteenth-century occult literature? Whatever you're interested in, there is probably a group near you organized around that interest. And where there's a group, there are people.

Again, the world is full of people who want to make contact. A significant proportion of them are available for sexual contact. If you feel open to this and are willing to reach these people, sexual contact is a regular and frequent result. That's how it works. Honestly.

# THIRTEEN

# Making Contact in Marriage (and Other Long-Term Relationships)

MARRIAGE AND OTHER FORMS of long-term intimate relationships present a set of problems somewhat different from the ones which we've discussed so far. While we have addressed the question of how to originate and establish contact, the marriage relationship presumes that a significant level of contact has already been achieved.

The marriage relationship raises questions about how two people can maintain and deepen their contact over a long period of time. The deterioration of contact in marriage is, in my estimate, the single most common marital problem, occurring more often than incidences of adultery, physical brutality, financial mismanagement, and sexual incompatibility combined. The painfully common story of modern marriage is of the wasting away of genuine contact until the relationship is only a hollow shell of what it once was, brittle and subject to fracture at the slightest pressure. How many American households, I wonder, contain two adults who share the same physical space, even the same bed, and yet have no idea of the thoughts, feelings, and day-to-day experiences of their partners?

This kind of loss of contact is deceptive; it creeps up on us without our realizing it. The very fact that we share the same physical space, eat meals together, have friends in common, sleep in the same bed, and own property together promotes the illusion of closeness long after any sharing of inner thoughts, feelings, and experiences has disappeared.

Here are some questions to consider that may help you assess the degree of contact you have in your relationship with your partner. There is no scoring system because none is relevant. It is for you alone to decide whether you are happy with your relationship as it now exists. Only you can say whether your needs for intimacy and contact are being fulfilled. Only you can decide whether you would like to change.

> How long has it been since you and your partner went out together, alone?
>
> How much time do you spend together just talking?
>
> Do you have sex frequently enough to satisfy you?
>
> How much time do you spend in "pseudocontact" (i.e., activity that looks like you are together, but really involves no sharing of thoughts and feelings, like TV watching, reading, working on projects)?
>
> When you talk together, how much of your talk is "business talk" (talk that deals with issues of the maintenance of household, children, possessions) as compared to "contact talk" (talk that involves the sharing of thoughts and feelings)?

Are there specific issues you don't feel free to discuss with your partner?

Are there feelings you do not feel free to express to your partner (e.g., anger, resentment, weakness, fear, need for closeness, need for sex—or even strong feelings of love!)?

How long has it been since one of you gave a gift to the other or did "something special" for the other for no reason other than affection?

How frequently do you touch one another, apart from having sex?

Could you recount, in general terms, how your partner spent his or her day apart from you? Could your partner do the same for you?

Our culture promotes the fallacy that love is a mysterious quality that appears and disappears spontaneously without rhyme or reason. Popular songs, magazine articles, phrases in our language (such as "head over heels in love" and "falling in love") all suggest that love is a force external to us. This view often seems appropriate for the intense emotional period of the courtship and the honeymoon, but it is a much more hazardous view in a long-term relationship. If love is a force over which we have no control, what happens when it "goes away"?

The fact of the matter is that "love" is an active verb denoting a set of rather complex but nevertheless specific behaviors. These specific behaviors are, I believe, a special case of contact behaviors involving two people and implying a sexual attraction between them. Love is a special form of contact in which the partners are saying to each other, "You are an important person to me. I am interested in who you are. I want to hear about your thoughts and feelings. I want to experience your body. I want to share your experience." By implication, each partner adds, "And I want you to feel the same way about me." It is this last message that distinguishes love from attraction or infatuation.

Even shy or socially unskillful people seem able to "fall in love" and many get married or form other long-term intimate relationships. The intensity of the courtship period can often alter the behavior of even the shyest person. But when the pairing has been achieved, the shy person's behavior has a tendency to return to normal—that is, noncontactful behavior comes back to the surface. As we say, often only half in jest, "the honeymoon is over."

Shy people, of course, are not the only ones who ease back to habitual behavior after marriage. The business or professional person returns to his or her preoccupation with career. The sports fanatic returns to Monday-night football. The socialite continues with community and organizational activities.

This "cooling off" is a natural development within limits. Few of us are rich enough either in time or emotional energy to sustain the kind of intense contact characteristic of courtship and honeymoon. Trouble occurs, however, when the withdrawal of one partner is so complete that real contact ceases. When this happens, the relationship goes "on a diet." If the relationship is healthy to begin with, it can survive on crumbs of contact for limited periods of time (as in wartime separations, or separations created by business relocations). But when the underrationing of contact is continued indefinitely, the relationship will develop malnutrition and eventually will die—in fact, if not in name.

Since a love relationship is a special case of contact between people, the contact behaviors described in earlier chapters are still applicable. Learning them is no major trick—it requires only time, practice, and willingness to change. The real trick is to employ these skills creatively in an intimate relationship to reverse any tendency toward deterioration of contact. Below are some suggestions that you may put to creative use in your relationship with your partner. They are intended as suggestions only. They most definitely are not a catalog of all the ways contact skills can be used in an intimate relationship. More ways, both planned and spontaneous, will suggest themselves to you. Almost without exception, each time you employ one of the contact behaviors you will increase the tendency toward a deeper, more meaningful relationship.

## *Verbal Attending Skills— How to Increase Your Partner's Interest in Talking with You*

The beginning of an intimate partnership is characterized by a mutual, active verbal approach of two people toward each other. Each is concerned and interested in learning what the other thinks and feels and who the other is. Many hours are spent in conversation, during which, piece by piece, the opinions, ideas, hopes, memories, and experiences of both come together. For each person, a more-or-less-complete picture of the other takes form. Once the pairing has been achieved, however, there comes a dropping off of verbal exploration.

How can you restimulate some of the conversation that provided both of you with so much contact during the period when you were coming together? First, let's look at the message you were transmitting during that period. All of your interest and curiosity in your partner's thoughts and feelings conveyed to him or her a very powerful statement, "You are important to me."

But as the relationship began to cool, your own concerns began to reassert their importance. Instead of expressing interest in the other's feelings, you became primarily involved with your own. Instead of wanting to hear his or her thoughts, it became more important for you to state yours. Instead of being aware of the other's experiences, you became preoccupied with your own. As these changes took place, the message you were conveying to your partner changed until you were saying, "You're not so important to me." Of course, as your partner experienced a lessening of his or her importance to you, he or she began to lose interest in your thoughts, feelings, and experiences.

To reverse this trend, begin to reintroduce messages that your partner's thoughts, feelings, and experiences *are* important to you. Very soon he or she will respond with a renewal of interest in you. How do you send these messages? Through ritual and information-seeking questions and active listening, with a few special adaptations to your particular relationship.

Ritual questions function as the initiators of contact, signaling your interest in the other person. To specify situations in which such questions might be used between married people seems to belabor the point, but it never ceases to amaze me how couples stop using ritual questions and then wonder why conversations don't get started. Some examples of when to use ritual questions are:

1. at the end of a day when you have been separated
2. after an activity that has prevented contact (an evening of TV, unshared home projects)
3. after a prolonged period of silence (as when driving long distances together)
4. following periods when the presence of other people has prevented contact (guests or children)

Remember that to convey the message that the partner is important, your ritual questions should ask about your partner; they should not be a prelude to a speech about yourself. Your ritual question at the end of a day of separation should be, "How was your day?" and not, "Was your day as hectic as mine?"

Information-seeking questions are naturally more specific in an intimate relationship than they would be in a more casual relationship. Many folks seem to get the idea, after they have been paired for a while, that there is no new information to be sought from their partner. I have had couples say to me with perfectly straight faces, "But we already know everything about each other! What could we possibly ask each other about?"

The notion is absurd. I believe that if we were to lock up any two adult human beings in a room together, it would be possible for them to talk about their experiences for the rest of their lives without running out of things to say. In a real-life situation, both partners have new experiences every day. The notion that your partner has nothing new to say is a symptom of being out of contact. No matter how long you and your partner have been together, there is probably a good deal that you don't know about him or her. For example:

What does he or she do every day? (I don't mean job title—I mean actual activities connected with work, where does he/she eat lunch, who are his/her friends?)

Do you understand the work your partner does?

What were your partner's "most" experiences (most embarrassing, most frightening, most exciting, etc.)?

What are your partner's hopes for the future?

What are your partner's political, religious, ethical views?

What about you does your partner dislike most? like most?

What was childhood like for your partner? What changes are happening with your partner?

Does your partner have a hobby? Do you understand it?

What would your partner name as his or her three biggest problems?

Once you have asked your question, active listening is the strongest statement you can make to your partner that his or her thoughts and feelings are important to you. When you actively listen to your partner (repeating the meaning of what he or she is saying to you), the message you are communicating is, "What you are saying is so interesting to me that I don't want to interrupt with my own comments. I just want to hear what you have to say and be sure I understand it."

Use active listening whenever your partner makes any substantive comment. Questions are designed to open conversation, but once a statement is made, active listening is the best tool to communicate your interest. Don't worry about whether your partner seems less interested in you than you are in him or her. Remember that if contact between you has decreased, your partner has devalued you as a source of pleasure. When you drag out of mothballs the contact skills we are describing, he or she will sooner or later respond with a renewed interest in you.

## Nonverbal Attending: The Body Language of Love

The nonverbal signals of contact remain the same in the context of an intimate partnership. They are the SOFTEN behaviors (see Chapter 6). Because there exists a sexual relationship between the partners, however, touching occupies a far more significant place in the nonverbal signals of love than it does in other forms of contact.

Diminished touching is one of the most striking indications a relationship is moving toward noncontact. At the beginning of the relationship, when both partners feel strong urges toward contact, touching is a common and frequently recurring behavior. The partners hold hands or put their arms around each other while walking. They hold hands over the restaurant table. The passenger touches the driver in the car. They kiss often as a spontaneous expression of caring.

As reversion toward noncontact sets in, shy people in particular may take a rather active role in discouraging touching, suddenly claiming that they "don't want to make a scene in public." Eventually, the partners are seldom touching one another at all except during sex. As might be predicted, the frequency of sex also diminishes rather drastically. (Touching and being touched are things that put us "in the mood" for sex. If touching is not happening, sexual desire has to come "out of the blue," which does happen, but not nearly so often as sexual desire that is stimulated.)

The other SOFTEN behaviors are still important, but their primary use is during conversation. Touching in the context of an intimate relationship is almost universally appropriate—that is, touching will promote contact between you and your partner almost every time you use it. Here are some brief pictures of how touching occurs in an intimate relationship in a nonsexual way that nevertheless promotes contact.

Paul and Jackie are up on a Saturday morning. Paul is working on the bills at his desk while Jackie reads the paper. Jackie gets up to refill her coffee cup, then refills Paul's. As she sets it on the desk, she puts her arm around his shoulder and kisses the top of his head. Without a word she returns to the sofa.

Gary comes home from work and Sue has not heard him come in. She is in the kitchen, preparing dinner. He hangs up his coat, then comes into the kitchen, and puts his arms around her and kisses the back of her neck. "Hi," he says. "How was your day?"

Greg and Tammy have evolved a little custom. Every night, after they turn out the light, he lies on his back and smokes a cigarette, while she lies on her side with her head on his shoulder and one arm across his body.

Chip is a physical therapist. It is his custom that whenever his wife, Nan, who is a lawyer, spends a full day in court, he gives her a massage that evening.

You may not want to talk with your partner about increasing the amount of touching you do. Try increasing your own frequency of touching silently. This will provide you with a striking demonstration of how physical touch can contribute to contact. Within a few days, if you are consistent, you will be amazed at the renewal of warmth and intimacy between you.

## Self-Disclosure in a Relationship

At the beginning of a relationship we struggle to show ourselves to the other, words tumbling over each other, ideas intertwining. But as we revert toward noncontact, we return to the closed, private world of our own thoughts, sharing less and less of ourselves with our partner. We each develop the illusion that we are fully known by the other, and that we fully know the other.

This is only an illusion; it could never be the truth. There is not enough time in our lives to share the total of our experiences even up to the present, and each of us is constantly changing and adding new experiences, both internal and external.

Many folks rationalize the loss of self-disclosure in their primary relationship by noting that the new thoughts, feelings, and experiences they could share with their partner are not important. The fact is that *contact is made in the sharing,* and not necessarily in what is shared. The act of self-disclosure is what is important to the process of making contact. When we tell each other the events of the day, it is not so much because the events were so interesting, but because we grow closer in the telling.

Although there is a section of exercises to promote contact at the end of this chapter, I want to single out the exercise immediately below because I believe it to be the most powerful formula to produce contact between lovers. I learned it from an older friend, a psychologist, who practiced it almost daily with his wife for more than twenty years. His only complaint was that it either extended itself because it was so interesting or it led to sex so frequently that he was often tired the next day.

## A Contact Exercise for Lovers

Set a time a half hour before bedtime (if you wish, you can expand the time period later). Turn off the TV, put away all reading matter, put down all handiwork. Soft background music is okay.

Prepare for each a serving of your favorite beverage.

For the first fifteen minutes designate one partner as the "talker" and the other partner as the "listener." The object of the talker is to share whatever comes to his or her mind in the way of thoughts and feelings. The object of the listener is simply to hear and understand the partner. The listener uses only ritual questions, information-seeking questions, and active listening, contributing none of his or her own thoughts, ideas, opinions, or suggestions.

After fifteen minutes reverse roles, so that the talker becomes the listener and the listener becomes the talker.

*Note:* Often the talking partner will feel he or she has nothing to say and will want to change roles before the time period has elapsed. Do not do so. If necessary, let that part of the time go by in silence. A relationship in which one person does all the talking is not a contact relationship.

## *Assertiveness:*
## *How Not to Destroy Your Contact with Repressed Anger*

The lapse toward noncontact we've been talking about is often brought on when one partner hides anger rather than expressing it. As this nonassertive partner becomes depressed and morose, noncontact behaviors begin showing up. Martha, who felt trapped by her husband and her four teen-aged sons, is a good example of this (see pages 130–132). The more trapped she felt, the higher the walls she put up around herself, keeping out her husband and her sons, making them not want to be in contact with her.

The way to avoid this repressed-anger pattern is to follow the three assertiveness behavior guidelines in Chapter 10. Again, they are:

1. The best way to get what you want is to ask for it.
2. The best way not to get what you don't want is to say no to it.
3. The best way to get someone to stop doing something you don't want them to do is to tell them how it makes you feel.

Let's look briefly at how these guidelines apply to the marriage or relationship situation.

The first guideline has to do with getting what you want. What do you want in your relationship, anyway? More companionship? More sex? More play? More communication? More financial responsibility? More friendships outside the relationship?

Whatever it is that you want, the most direct route to getting it is to ask for it. Start out by admitting that what you want is *your* responsibility. It's not your partner's responsibility either to read your mind or even to agree to your wishes once you've expressed them.

Marriage counselors often hear stories of a partner in a marriage or relationship who feels angry, resentful, "unfaired against" because the partner doesn't fulfill the needs and wants he or she feels. After all, the patient asks, shouldn't a husband (or wife) be interested in sex? Doesn't he have a right to expect a clean house when he comes home from a full day of work? Aren't marriage partners supposed to share their deepest thoughts and feelings? Isn't my partner wrong to behave as he or she does? The answer to each of these questions is no.

All that has really been established is that the complaining partner wants more sex, a cleaner house, or better communication. When you come to the point where you see that it is your needs, and not your partner's deficiencies, that raise the issue, then you are in a position to do something about it. The thing to do, of course, is to ask for what you want. These principles will help you phrase your requests.

1. Acknowledge your responsibility for what you want by making use of "I language." When you say, "I want," you allow your partner to respond to your wishes because he or she cares for you. When you say, "You should," you imply that there is something wrong with his or her behavior, and if your partner responds to your wishes, he or she is merely "obeying you," rather than making a free choice. If your partner gives in to "demands" rather than "requests," he or she is giving up the right to choose freely.

2. Be specific in your requests. If you can see that your partner is not clearly aware of what you want, or how to accomplish what you want, then it is up to you to make yourself as clear as possible.

Here are some examples of how to and how not to use "I language," and specifically to ask for what you want:

Not I LANGUAGE: "Why do you have to read that damned newspaper over breakfast every morning?

TOO VAGUE: "I wish you'd talk with me more."

CORRECT: "I'd really like it if we could talk together during breakfast, and you'd read the paper at another time."

Not I LANGUAGE: "Your problem is you have an abnormal disinterest in sex."

TOO VAGUE: "I wish you were more affectionate."

CORRECT: "I really feel a need and a desire to have sex with you more often than we have been."

Similarly, we often hear the complaints of nonassertive partners who have not learned the truth of guideline 2—"The best way not to get what you don't want is to say no to it." For extremely nonassertive people, the idea that they have the right to say no is dumbfounding. Witness the following conversation I had with a patient:

PATIENT: "My husband has this sick attachment to his mother and I suffer for it!"

THERAPIST: "Oh? How do you suffer for it?"

PATIENT: "Well, every Sunday afternoon we have to go over to her house and visit her. It drives me crazy! The old woman is the nastiest, most critical . . ."

THERAPIST: "Excuse me, but by 'we' do you mean you and your husband?"

PATIENT: "Sure."

THERAPIST: "Well, if you're right about *his* sick attachment to his mother, I can see why *he* would have to go, but I don't see how it follows that *you* have to go."

PATIENT: "That's it, you see! That's why it's so unfair! I mean, he just says, 'Well, it's about time we were getting over to Mother's,' without even asking me. I don't call that very fair, do you?"

THERAPIST: "Maybe I'm not understanding, but I still don't see how all that means *you* have to go."

PATIENT: "Well, he tells his mother *we'll* be there, and so she expects me to be there."

THERAPIST: "So you mean that the fact that he told his mother you'd be there means you 'have to go'?"

PATIENT: "Of course . . . well, no, but if I didn't go she'd be angry."

THERAPIST: "So what you really mean is that in order to keep her from getting angry you 'have to go'?"

PATIENT: (pause) "I guess it's not disappointing her so much as it is that he expects me to go."

THERAPIST: "So you choose to go so as not to disappoint him?"

PATIENT: (angrily) "No! I don't *choose* to go!"

THERAPIST: "But the fact that your husband expects you to go means that you 'have to go'?"

PATIENT: (uncertain now) "Nooo, I . . . that doesn't make too much sense, does it?"

THERAPIST: "I wonder if it might be that you really don't 'have to go' at all?"

This patient and I practiced some ways that she could say no to the next Sunday's visit. She set up a date to play tennis on Sunday afternoon with her friend, and when she told her husband, his reaction was predictably angry: "But we always go to Mother's on Sunday afternoon." She replied (as we had rehearsed), "Yes, I've always gone with you, but the truth is, I haven't enjoyed it much for a while now, and I've even gotten to resent it. I've decided that I am willing to go with you twice a month. If you want to go every Sunday, that's your privilege, and I'll just plan something else." Eventually, her husband also cut down his visits to two per month. Her assertiveness also brought the side benefit of giving her and her husband more time together.

The third assertiveness guideline—"The best way to get someone to stop doing something you don't like is to tell him or her how it makes you feel"—is designed to provide your partner with a reason for changing his or her behavior. When a person habitually goes through a given behavior, you may assume that (a) that's the way he prefers to do things, and (b) he sees no good reason not to do things that way. If you tell him that there is something wrong with his behavior, and to change it, he may (a) not agree with your judgment of wrongness, and (b) resent being told what to do. If, however, you tell him how his behavior bothers you, without implying that there is anything wrong with the behavior itself, he is far more likely to be willing to change it simply because it bothers you.

For example, your husband, when getting ready for bed, meticulously hangs up all his clothes, places his shoes in the closet, and then drops his dirty socks at the foot of the bed. He's done this every night of your marriage and it drives you crazy. You can respond:

INCORRECT: "You slob! I've been watching you drop your cruddy socks on the floor every night for five years, and it's disgusting!"

CORRECT: "George, I know you've dropped your socks at the foot of the bed all your life. I really should have told you this long ago, but it really bothers me a lot. I always put them in the hamper the next day, but it makes me feel like a hired maid to do it. Would you mind putting them in the hamper yourself when you get undressed?" (Then, if you obtain agreement) "And since I know it's a strong habit for you, may I have your permission to remind you when you forget?"

### EXERCISES

Below are some suggestions you may find helpful in bringing greater contact into your marriage or relationship. See how many you can add to the list.

### Social

These exercises are particularly effective in creating contact if they are *not* used on a birthday or other special occasion.

1. Arrange to go out (just the two of you) to a nice restaurant for dinner. Pick an evening when you know your partner is free, and surprise him or her. Pick the restaurant yourself, make the reservations, and pick up the bill (that can be particularly delightful if the man is the partner being surprised).

2. Have some flowers delivered to your partner at home or at work. (Yes, women, many men do like flowers.)

3. Make something with your own hands for your partner.

4. Go for a walk together.

5. Find something that neither of you has ever done before and give it a try (going skiing or to the opera, eating at a Congolese restaurant, going on an overnight hike, etc.).

**Verbal Attending**
6. Practice asking a ritual question:

    a. when your partner (or you) gets home from work
    b. when you sit down to dinner
    c. when you get up in the morning

7. See how much you can get your partner to tell you by asking information-seeking questions about:

    a. his or her job
    b. his or her hobby
    c. his or her major field of study in college or trade school
    d. his or her childhood

8. Establish a "talking only" time with each of you communicating half of the time period, as described on page 199.

**Nonverbal Attending**
9. Reread Chapter 6. Memorize the SOFTEN list. Start by performing all six behaviors once while you are together. Now try to raise the score by one each time until you can go through the list ten times while you are together.
10. Make a list of ways you can express nonsexual

affection for your partner by touching. Start (without telling your partner what you're doing) by trying to touch him or her once every two hours while you're together. Then go to once every hour. After one week, try to touch your partner once every half hour.

Though exercises 9 and 10 sound quite artificial and mechanical, they are extremely useful in measuring and regulating the increases in your nonverbal contact behaviors. The results are electrifying!

### Self-Disclosure

11. Reread Chapter 8 and see how many of the exercises you can adapt to fit your relationship with your partner.

12. Tell your partner an experience of your day while you were apart.

13. Tell your partner about a book that you've read. (It might even be this one!)

14. During the "talking only" time (page 199), arrange to tell about your "most" experiences: happiest, saddest, etc.

15. At an unexpected moment tell your partner that you love him or her.

16. Discuss what you feel to be your biggest problem with your partner.

17. Tell one of the things you like the most about your partner.

### Assertiveness

18. Identify something that you want from your relationship but are not getting. Now imagine the specific behavior or behaviors that your partner could use to

provide that something. Now practice, in front of a mirror, asking for it, using "I language" and making clear *specifically* what you would like. When you are satisfied with your request, put it to your partner.

19. Identify something that your partner does that bothers you. When you speak to him or her about it,

    a.   identify specifically what he or she is doing
    b.   describe how it makes you feel when he or she does it
    c.   specify an alternative behavior that would be satisfactory to you

Preserving intimacy, contact, and love throughout a marriage or relationship *is* possible, but it does not happen automatically. It happens when a very specific set of behaviors, contact behaviors, are consistently performed by both partners.

It may be that you have been wondering lately whether the relationship you are in is worth the trouble anymore. If you are very sure that it is not, and that you are emotionally finished with the relationship, then it probably makes sense to end it cleanly rather than to try to resurrect its remains for nostalgic reasons or from a feeling of duty. But if there remains any vestige of the interest, attraction, and caring that initially drew you together, try the techniques described in this chapter. They'll give a revitalizing charge to the attraction that drew you together in the first place.

# FOURTEEN

# Making Contact in
# Social Situations—A Review

SOCIAL SITUATIONS—parties, dates, visiting, group activities—exist because they are fun. They are direct expressions of our human need to be together. While we are brought together with other people for a wide variety of tasks—school, work, etc.—social events are an expression of the joy of being together just for its own sake.

But social situations are no fun for shy people. Depending on the degree of their shyness, they may feel anything from a mild sense of restlessness and uncertainty to such extreme physical reactions as heart palpitations, nausea, and even fainting. The plight of the shy person is a little like that of a person with *anorexia nervosa,* a neurotic inability to eat. Such a person knows he will starve if he doesn't eat, yet he panics at the sight of food. The shy person knows that he or she needs contact with others in order to be happy, but panics in potential contact situations.

The two following accounts of a hypothetical shy person at a party represent the alternatives that are open to you. On one hand, you can hang on to your negative self-image and the behaviors it brings on, resulting in the self-imprisonment we call shyness. On the other, you can re-form your self-image and change the behaviors that have contributed to your shyness. The methods and techniques for making contact that are described in this book have been proven effective, but they depend on your willingness to use them and to dare to change your old behavior for new.

In the first of these accounts Britt suffers from a fairly severe degree of shyness. In the second account she has spent considerable time and energy practicing the techniques presented in this book to overcome her shyness. As you read the two accounts, you may note similarities to your own experiences as a shy person and as a person working to overcome your shy behavior. As you note the specific techniques Britt uses in the second account, look back to Chapters 4 through 8 for help in developing these techniques yourself. I hope Britt's experience in improving her contact with other people and overcoming her shyness will be your experience too.

### The Party—I

"Please God," thought Britt, "don't let this be another absolute disaster." As the time of tonight's party drew near, her memory called up images of one embarrassing incident after another at parties she had attended in the past. After the party last year with Mark's old University friends, she'd firmly resolved never to accept another invitation to a party ever again. But when Dolores had called, well, she couldn't very well decline an invitation from practically the best friend she'd ever had, even if they had gone their separate ways after college graduation three years ago.

Britt smiled to herself as she thought of Dolores. Cute, pixyish, and effervescent, Dolores always seemed to be in the middle of a crowd no matter where she was. They were an unlikely pair of friends. Britt was tall, fair, blonde, and Scandinavian, while Dolores was tiny, dark, and Mediterranean. When she was around Dolores, Britt recalled, she felt even more like the great, dumb dairy cow that she usually felt like. Dolores was popular, too. She'd probably turned down three times as many dates as Britt had had in college.

Britt grimaced as she remembered the time Dolores accepted a date on the condition that her date find a guy for Britt and they double. The poor guy had really tried hard to make conversation, she recalled, but had finally given up when she'd only been able to sit and stare at her immense feet and mumble one-word replies. He'd spent the rest of the evening in a three-way conversation with Dolores and her date.

"Well," Britt thought, looking firmly at her image in the mirror, "I'll do better tonight. My God, I have to! Or will I? I'm not sure I even know Dolores anymore, let alone anyone else who'll be there." Dolores had called as soon as she had moved back to town to begin her year of internship at a local hospital, and they had had lunch together. Britt had found herself ashamed of her job as a dental hygienist and had a hard time relating to Dolores as a soon-to-be physician. They'd avoided their discomfort by nostalgically recalling their college years, but a continuous thread of uneasiness had

run through the entire luncheon. Dolores had not
called again, until now.

"Oh, no!" she thought, noticing with consternation
the beginnings of a pimple forming just below her
lower lip. "That's all I need! In an hour I'll look like a
refugee from the clown's makeup room at the circus.
That's the first thing anyone who talks to me is going to
notice. If my clutzy body doesn't turn them off, this
surely will!"

Looking at the clock and seeing it was nearly time to
leave, Britt vainly tried to fight down a rising sense of
panic. With trembling fingers, she lit a cigarette just to
kill some time. She wanted to be sure not to be among
the first to arrive, so as to avoid that awful, uneasy time
when only two or three guests tried somehow to get
things going.

As she studied the rising ribbon of smoke, her
thoughts mercilessly returned to the disasters of parties
past. She thought again of the party last year with
Mark's fraternity friends, and how her tongue had sat
like a lump of yesterday's oatmeal in her mouth. It had
been an evening of pure agony as she sat dumbly next
to Mark, trying to think of some clever response to the
jovial conversation of Mark's friends and their dates.
She remembered with burning shame listening to
Mark's frustrated and angry outburst after the party.
"Small wonder," she thought, "that he never called me
again."

Then there was the high school pregraduation party
that Lars, her twin brother, had insisted on having at
their house. That one almost worked out, she thought
wryly. The group, a combination of Lars's football

teammates and her honor society friends, had actually
meshed pretty well. She had found that playing the role
of hostess had actually helped her feel easier. Late in
the evening she had even become comfortable enough
to sit at the edge of a small group who were discussing
their plans after graduation. And then, she recalled, her
cheeks flushing with embarrassment at the memory,
her parents came home from their evening at the Elk's
club. She remembered, with the clarity of a motion
picture, how Daddy had stood in the entrance hall star-
ing muzzily around the group, taken two steps, and
passed out in an alcoholic stupor on the living room
floor! The guests had left in an apologetic silence, leaving her and Lars and Mother to get him into bed.

Her mind flashed back even further, to the party her
mother had had for her kindergarten friends on her
sixth birthday. Like it was yesterday! She'd felt so
happy, so expectant. They'd all brought her little presents and sung "Happy Birthday," and she'd blown out
her candles . . . and then they were playing a form of
charades, and laughing uproariously, when above all
the childish laughter Billy Kiefert's voice had shrilled,
"Oooh, look, Britt wet her pants." Looking down in
horror, she saw and felt the warm, spreading stain dark-
ening her beautiful powder-blue dress and the beige
carpet. To make matters worse, her mother had made
her change, not to another dress but to her corduroy
coveralls, because she "couldn't be trusted," and then
made her go back to the party. All that year in kindergarten, to her shame, the other kids called her "pissy-
pants."

She stubbed out her cigarette and checked the mir-

ror one last time, and noted that the pimple seemed to
have turned scarlet and grown to the size of a half-
dollar. "Well," she thought, "might as well face the
music."

Her depression deepened in the car on the way.
"Damn it all," she thought, "it isn't fair! Why did I have
to be born shy? It's like a birth defect—worse, even,
because when you're physically handicapped, people
make allowances. But when you're socially handicapped, people think you're a big turkey. I guess the
best thing is just to accept that I'll never be anything
other than stupid and clumsy in social settings."

Walking up the steps to Dolores's front door, she
almost turned around. She could claim illness or car
trouble and just not show up. She paused a moment,
debating, when the door burst open and there was
Dolores, arms open, saying, "Britt! I'm so glad you
could come! Hey, everybody, meet my old college
roomie, Britt Olsen!"

"I, uh, I brought some wine," Britt said, holding out
the package.

"Great," said Dolores. "Here, I'll take it out to the
kitchen while you get acquainted," and before Britt
could protest she was gone.

"Now what in God's name should I do?" Britt
thought, feeling a momentary flash of anger toward
Dolores for stranding her like this. "She knows I'm a
social dud. Why couldn't she at least try to make things
a bit easier for me?"

She wandered a bit, pretending to study the bric-a-
brac on the shelves. Covertly, she looked around at the
group. Young people mostly, twenty-five to early thir-

ties, she guessed. Men bearded and long-haired, girls in blue jeans, one in a suede pants suit. Suddenly her floor-length dark green velour dress seemed hopelessly out of place.

". . . So Markham says, 'Prepare me a hypo of 15 cc's of salicylic acid, nurse,' and she says, 'But Doctor, we've got a great big bottle of aspirin right out at the desk!' " she overheard a man saying to a group sitting near the fireplace, who all began to laugh. "Oh, I should have known—other medical students," Britt realized. "I shouldn't have come. I'm just so out of place here!"

"Hi, there," said a voice directly behind her.

Turning, she cast a quick glance upward to see a dark beard surrounding a smiling mouth. Impression of dark curly hair and warm brown eyes. Nice eyes.

"Hello," she replied, looking down at the drink in her hand.

"I'm Dan. Dan Wittley."

"Nice to meet you," she said. She felt frozen, stiff. "Please help," she thought to herself, "someone help!"

He paused a moment. "Well, uh, what's your name?"

"I'm Britt Olsen."

"Oh yeah," he smiled. "You were Dolores's college roommate, isn't that right?"

"Yes . . ." Now what? She turned, pretending to study the painting hanging on the wall near her. "I've got to think of something to say," she thought, mind racing.

"Well . . . what do you do now, Britt?" Dan asked, sounding a bit uncertain of himself.

Britt turned and half-faced him, "Well, I'm just a dental hygienist."

"Oh."

Out of the corner of her eye, Britt stole a glance at
Dan. He was beginning to look uncomfortable now,
shifting his weight from one foot to the other. He ran
a hand through his curly hair.

"Do you like it?" he asked.

"Like what?"

"Well . . . dental hygiene."

"Oh. It's pretty boring, I guess."

Dan was looking around uneasily now. "Uh, I guess
I should go see if I can set out the dip or something,"
he said, and walked off.

"I knew I shouldn't have come," Britt thought, tears
of humiliation stinging her eyes. "I mean, it's dumb to
expect any two strangers, let alone a clod like me, to
have much to say to one another." A dull sense of lonely
despair began to settle over her.

"So how've you been, kiddo?" Dolores's voice summoned her out of her gloom.

"Oh, okay, I guess. How 'bout you?"

"God, you wouldn't believe it, Britt! My life's just a
whirlwind! Six months I've been in town already and I
haven't even got all my stuff unpacked! Between seminars, hospital duties, and fending off horny interns, I
haven't got time to sleep! Hey, is there a main man in
your life yet?"

"Oh, no, I . . ."

A voice interrupted. "Dee, let me take you away
from all of this liberated-lady-doctor stuff and keep you
barefoot and pregnant while I earn fat fees for remov-
ing chins from aging debutantes." The deep voice belonged to a good-looking man in a silk shirt printed with
an impressionist design. He swept a long arm around

Dolores and pulled her toward the group near the fireplace.

"See you later, Britt," called Dolores over her shoulder, "after I try to save the soul of this social parasite!"

Britt watched Dolores move off with a poignant sense of loss. She'd never be like Dolores: sure of herself, popular, always knowing exactly what to say. It had seemed not so bad when she and Dolores had been close, but now it seemed clear that Dolores had outgrown her, and Britt felt very alone.

"One more glass of wine," she thought, "and I can make a graceful exit." As she passed through the kitchen to refill her glass, she overheard two women talking about skiing, the one sport she really enjoyed.

"The one thing I miss about the ski slopes in this area," said one, "is that there don't seem to be any areas with really long intermediate-level runs."

"Well, yeah," said the other, "I think that's because the mountains out here are so steep and rugged, where the mountains back east are older and gentler."

Britt had an impulse to join them and tell the first woman about her favorite area where there were several broad, gentle runs. She hesitated, then shrugged to herself. "They don't want a stranger busting into their conversation. Anyway, I'd probably make an ass of myself, like with Dan." She turned sideways and squeezed behind the second woman so as not to pass between them.

In the living room she spotted an overstuffed wingback chair in a corner and curled up in it, holding her glass of wine and trying to look unconcerned about being alone. Several small groups had collected, and she could hear snatches of several conversations. They all seemed so . . . connected, somehow. What was wrong with her that she couldn't be like that?

"Hey, Britt," called Dolores from the group near the fire, "c'mon over and join us."

"Oh, that's okay, I . . ." she began.

*"C'mon,"* said Delores, more insistently. Britt hesitantly got up from her chair and squeezed in, next to Dolores, on the floor near the fire. "Fritz Ross, Barbara, Dick Haines," she named, pointing an introductory finger at each, "this is Britt." She nodded to the group.

"Here you go," said Haines, holding out to her a cigarette with an odd, pointy-ended shape. "Oh, my God," Britt thought, "it's marijuana! What do I do now? I don't want to seem stuffy, but I'm afraid of that stuff." She took the cigarette, put it to her lips, and pretended to draw on it, as she had seen the others do. She noticed Haines smiling quietly at her, and with a flush of embarrassment realized she hadn't fooled him, or anyone else either, probably. "I can't do anything right," she moaned inwardly.

"Britt's a dental hygienist," Dolores said brightly to no one in particular. "How embarrassing," Britt thought. "She's trying to draw me into the group." Feeling the flush creeping up her neck, she folded her arms and looked intently at her feet. With a sudden sense of relief, she noticed her wine glass was almost empty. She drained it, and said to Delores, "Hey, thanks for inviting me, but I've got to work in the morning." It wasn't true, but it was a way out.

"Well," said Dolores, "let's get together soon, huh?"

On her way home in the car, Britt thought, "I will

absolutely never, ever, accept an invitation to a party again."

## *The Party—II*

"I guess," thought Britt, "that I can look at tonight as a chance to try to put all the stuff I've been working on to the test." Her memory called up images of embarrassing events from past parties, and she felt a sense of anxiety tightening her throat. "Hold it," she told herself firmly. "Dwelling on those memories is a good way to talk myself into a disaster tonight." After the party last year that had led to the break-up with Mark, she'd resolved never to accept another invitation to a party. But that was before she'd picked up that book about shyness, and discovered that there were some things she could do about her problem. When Dolores, her former college roommate, had called to invite her to the party, it had seemed like a good chance to use all the "contact skills" she'd been learning. Feeling a bit scared, she'd nevertheless promised Dolores she'd be there.

Britt smiled to herself as she thought of Dolores. Cute, pixyish, effervescent, popular, always seeming to be in the middle of a crowd. Britt saw that Dolores was the perfect contrasting background against which she could focus on all her "negative subjective truths." Maybe, she thought ironically, that's what had made them friends. When she was around Dolores, it made it easier to see herself as a big, stupid cow. It fit right in with her negative program.

"Well, I'm through with that program," she re-

minded herself, and just for good measure, recited a bit
of the positive self-description she had made up to
"change the way she talked to herself." Closing her
eyes, she murmured, "I'm a competent and attractive
adult woman. I have my Scandinavian genes to thank
for a body some people would call statuesque. I really
like my blue eyes, blonde hair, and regular features. I
look like me, and I'm glad, because I like who I am."

She shook her head ruefully as she thought back to
her college years. That damned negative self-image
had been the source of so much trouble for her. She'd
huddled in fear inside herself, afraid at every moment
that she'd make an ass of herself and that someone
would discover what an absolute clod she was. Even the
memory of it was painful. She had been so afraid, and
so alone. "It took twenty-five years," she thought, "but
at least I'm doing something about it now."

"It'll be different tonight," she resolved, "because I
know how to make it different." She used to think of
her shyness as a curse, as if it were some peculiar kink
in her personality that made it difficult to make contact
with people. Now she understood that being shy had
nothing to do with who she was—she had been shy
because of what she had been doing when she was
around other people, and now, thank God, she knew
how to do some things differently. She wondered if
Dolores would be surprised.

"Damn," she said, noticing the beginnings of a pimple forming below her mouth. A pang of anxiety flashed
through her, and then she smiled. Not so long ago she
would have felt that that pimple would disgust everyone who looked at her. "How could I have been so

self-important?" she wondered. She had spent some time now testing the proposition in the shyness book that "each person stands at the center of his own universe" and had found it accurate. She knew that if she used the methods she had learned to acknowledge the importance of other people's experiences, no one would even begin to notice the tiny inflammation on her skin.

Finishing her makeup, she glanced at the clock and saw that it was nearly time to leave. Just enough time for a quick session of relaxation and imagining. She lay down on the bed, and drawing a series of slow, deep breaths, began to relax each muscle of her body in turn, starting with her toes all the way up to the muscles of her face. Completely relaxed, she reached over to the night table and pressed the "play" button on her cassette tape player. In a moment she heard her own voice, soft, slow, soothing.

"I'm a competent, attractive adult woman. I have my Scandinavian genes to thank for a body some people would call statuesque. I like my blue eyes, blonde hair, and regular features. I look like me, and I'm glad, because I like who I am.

"Who I am is a woman of twenty-five, an able and skilled dental hygienist. I enjoy skiing in particular, and being out of doors generally. More than that, I am a person who likes people. Every day I find I am more appreciative of and interested in the thoughts, feelings, and experiences of others. And as that appreciation and interest grows, I'm finding that other people like and appreciate me."

As the words sank into her relaxed mind, Britt began

to feel more and more anticipation for the party tonight. It would be a time, she thought, to explore other
people, perhaps to share some of herself with them,
maybe even make a new friend . . .

The buzz of the alarm clock warned her that it was
time to leave. As she put on her outer clothes, Britt
reflected that it was no wonder that parties were a
special problem for her. What a history of trauma!
From her sixth birthday party, when she had wet her
pants, to that awful graduation party she and Lars had
given, she saw how she had become conditioned to
expect a disaster at a party. Given that history, one
could almost have predicted that she would be frozen
in fear at the party with Mark last year. Well, whether
it was bad luck or fate that had caused her to have those
experiences, she knew that they were in the past and
she could let them go.

In the car on the way, Britt began to review in her
mind the specific kinds of contact skills she'd been practicing for several months now. "Conversation," she recited mentally, "has at least three elements: ritual questions, which are really symbols, like a handshake in
words." She paused in her outlining to smile at the
rearview mirror. "How are you? What do you do? What
a pretty dress you're wearing!" Then, she thought,
there are the information-seeking questions. Use them
during a conversation to show you're interested and
want to know more, but only as a spur to conversation
at a pause. Mostly, use active listening responses.

"Funny," she thought, "how effective that active listening method is." When she'd first read about it in the
shyness book, she'd thought it was really stupid. She

couldn't imagine trying to parrot back the sense of what other people said to her and passing that off as intelligent conversation. But when she'd tried it out, the results had really surprised her. People didn't seem to notice that she really wasn't contributing anything original to the dialogue. Instead, they really opened up. The other surprise was how she felt when she listened actively. All of a sudden she wasn't worried about what to say. Instead, she found herself really understanding how the other person felt about things. Active listening had felt a little awkward at first, but she'd been amazed at how easy it was once she got the hang of it.

"Then there are the nonverbal signals," she recalled. They had been a little trouble at first, not because they were so hard to understand, but because they felt so strange. It wasn't until she'd actually tried some of the exercises that she'd realized how habitually she'd been using all the "wrong" signals—no eye contact, a dead-pan face, huddled and closed body postures. Because of her long-established habits of using "shy" nonverbal signals, using the "right" signals for contact had felt funny, uncharacteristic, and even uncomfortable at first.

"Let's see," she reminded herself, "for openers, in choosing a place to sit or a path to walk, be among people, not around them. Then, SOFTEN." Taking a breath, she recited, "S–smile, O–open posture, F–forward lean, T–touch, E–eye contact, N–nod." Once she'd gotten over feeling uncomfortable about sending those nonverbal signals, she'd found it fairly easy to run through the list in her mind while talking with someone. And the results had been incredible! She'd found that people responded to the nonverbal signals like a blossom responded to the sun.

"Then there's self-disclosure," she thought, continuing her mental review. "Self-disclosure is, by definition, letting other people in on my experience." Like the other contact skills, self-disclosure had been initially difficult for Britt. She'd had to fight all the old negative thoughts that other people would find her self-disclosures trivial, stupid, and boring. She composed a job description, which had not been hard because her job was similar to the one given as an example in the book. She'd rehearsed telling a joke and several stories about her life. Britt smiled now as several incidents involving Dolores and herself occurred to her. They might serve as useful self-disclosures at this party, if the right moment came.

"I probably won't have to use assertiveness tonight," she reflected, "but I'll review it again anyway. First," she listed out loud, " 'The best way to get what you want is to ask for it.' Second, 'The best way not to get what you don't want is to say no to it!' Third, 'The best way to get someone to stop doing something you don't like is to tell them how it affects you.' " She still felt that she wasn't too good on assertiveness yet. The situations seemed to happen so fast that she didn't have time to think out an appropriate response. "At least," she mused wryly, "I've progressed far enough to see what I should have said. Maybe that Assertiveness Training course at the community college will help me become quicker on the draw."

Walking up the steps to Dolores's front door, her insides contracted with a wave of anxiety. She recognized her impulse to escape. She paused on the porch, closed her eyes, and drew several deep breaths, which she had learned immediately countered the physical effects of anxiety. She started to repeat some positive thoughts when the door flew open.

"Britt! I'm so glad you could come." It was Dolores, smiling, arms extended and open. SOFTEN! flashed through Britt's mind and, smiling, she moved forward with her own arms extended and hugged Dolores. "I'm glad, too. How are you?"

"Fine, fine," Dolores said, "c'mon in and meet the folks. Hey, everybody, meet Britt Olsen, my old college roomie!"

Britt felt a little tension as the guests looked at her, but she smiled and, looking each person momentarily in the eyes, nodded briefly to each. "Hi," she said to the group in general. To Dolores, "Where can I put this wine?"

"Here, I'll take it while you get acquainted," Dolores said, and before Britt could protest, she was gone. Britt remembered, standing uncertainly in the entryway, the first rule of nonverbal signaling, "Get among people." Taking a deep breath to relax herself, she moved into the living room and sat down on the sofa between two others. A young bearded man was telling an apparently funny story about a fellow intern and a nurse and aspirin. She felt momentarily intimidated as she realized these must be Dolores's medical student friends, but she knew she would be acting shyly if she made no move at all toward making contact with them. "Let's see," she thought, as the group's laughter died down. "Conversation—ritual question."

"Are you all interns?" she asked, smiling and looking at the eyes of the storyteller.

"No, uh . . ."

"Britt," she supplied.

"Britt," he said, smiling. "I'm an intern, and so is Haines, here. Dick, Fritz, and Ross," he said, and she nodded and smiled toward each, "are third-year students, and Barbara, though I'll never know why, is Ross's wife."

Barbara laughed. "Allen disapproves of marriage, Britt. I think he's afraid it'd interfere with his social life!"

Again, as the laughter died down, there was a momentary pause. "Information-seeking question," Britt thought.

Looking at Ross, she asked, "What's the difference between third year and internship?"

"Well," he said, looking pleased that she'd asked, "we're on a series of sort of mini-internships, called rotations, in which we get some practical experience in each of the services over the course of the year."

"So," she said, remembering how to respond as an active listener, "you kind of move around and get to sample different branches of hospital practice?"

"Exactly," he replied. "The idea is not only to train us in a variety of medical procedures, but also to help us gain information to decide which branch of medicine to pick as a specialty."

She was about to ask if Ross had picked a specialty yet, when Dolores's voice came from the kitchen. "Hey, Britt," she called, "can you give me a hand serving this wine?"

" 'Scuse me," she said to the group, "duty calls."

She helped Dolores distribute glasses of wine, and then stood uncertainly in the dining room, wondering what to do next. The group in the living room had seemed pretty friendly and she'd seemed to be doing pretty well at using contact skills with them. She was just about to rejoin them, when a voice said, "Hi, there," almost directly behind her.

Turning, she looked up into the eyes of a very tall man with curly brown hair and beard. The eyes were brown also, and warm and friendly.

"Hello," she replied, smiling, "I'm Britt Olsen." It popped out of her quite naturally, and she was suddenly grateful for the practicing she'd done in introducing herself.

"I'm Dan. Dan Wittley." He paused, seemed a bit uncertain.

Britt tensed suddenly with a flash of old panic. She found this Dan quite attractive. "Steady there, girl," she told herself, drawing a deep breath. "Let's do it by the book. Ritual question first."

"It's nice to meet you, Dan. Are you a medical person too?"

"Oh no," he laughed, suddenly seeming to relax a bit, "actually I'm an assistant manager of the Valu-spot Supermarket over near the University. I'm one of Dolores's neighbors upstairs. How about you?"

"I'm a dental hygienist. I work with a dentist over in Mayfield."

"That's interesting," Dan said. "Do you like it?"

He must have read the same book I did, Britt thought. Her mind flashed to the job description she had written. "I really do," she answered, "I get to meet and interact with a lot of people, and at the same time I get a sense of competence with a pretty technical set of skills." Back to him now, she thought. "How do you feel about your job?"

He paused. "I'm not sure, I guess. My real thing is painting, but I figured out a long time ago that it was going to be awhile before I sold enough paintings to live on, so I looked for something that'd make me a living without taking too much out of me. The grocery store seems to do that, but it isn't the thrill of a lifetime."

"What kind of paintings do you do?" Britt asked.

"Images of myths," Dan replied, getting excited. "I got involved in it reading Jung's works. He convinced me that myths are really important in shaping people's lives. Right now I'm working on a series of paintings based on the book *The Golden Bough*. Do you know it?"

"Only from a classics class in college," Britt answered. "Your paintings sound fascinating. Maybe I'll get to see one someday."

Dan hesitated, uncertain. "I'd like for you to see them. I don't find it easy to talk to many people, but it's really easy to talk to you, Britt. Maybe you wouldn't mind if I called you sometime, and we went out?"

Dan *was* shy, she realized, noticing him looking at the floor uncomfortably. She reached out and touched his arm. "I'd really like that very much. Got a pen? I'm at HA 7–6950."

"Hey, thanks, Britt." He smiled warmly. "I'll call you soon, huh? Right now, it's eleven thirty and I've got to work in the morning, so I better get going. I'm really looking forward to seeing you again."

"Eleven thirty!" Britt mused as Dan moved off. "Funny how time used to turn into eternity at parties. I can't believe this. I'm actually enjoying myself, and I sat in a group and actually talked, and I just made a date with a really attractive guy! I guess," she thought, remembering a principle from the book she'd read, "shyness really is all in the way you behave."

"So how've you been, kiddo?" Dolores's voice summoned her out of her clouds of thought.

"Really good, Dolores," she replied. "How about you?"

"You wouldn't believe it," Dolores laughed. "My life's a whirlwind, between hospital duties, seminars, and fending off horny interns, I don't even have time to sleep! I'm sorry I haven't gotten back to you since last time, but things have been just so crazy with my schedule."

Britt took a deep breath. She'd felt disappointed for months now with how her lunch with Dolores had gone. She'd rehearsed in her mind a statement that was a combination of self-disclosure and assertiveness that she had wanted to say to Dolores, and now was clearly the time to make it. "Dolores, about the time we had lunch. I was kind of uncomfortable and intimidated by knowing that you were almost a doctor. I felt like I let my shyness get in the way of our reestablishing our friendship. There're a lot of changes in my life I want to share with you. What I'd like is, as soon as your schedule allows, for us to have lunch again, okay?"

Dolores's expression sobered, and there were tears in

her eyes. "For sure. I was disappointed after our lunch
too. I kept wondering, 'Where did my friend Britt go?'
and . . ." Dolores reached out and touched her arm, "I
want her back as my friend."

Britt and Dolores hugged each other briefly. "Hey,"
said Dolores, "c'mon in by the fire." Taking Britt's
hand, Dolores led her into the living room. Around the
fire were several of the group she'd met when she first
arrived. She sat down in the circle before the fire, next
to Dolores.

"Here you go," said Haines, holding out to her a
cigarette with an odd, pointy-ended shape. "Oh, my
God," she thought, "it's marijuana! What do I do now?
I don't want to seem stuffy, but I'm scared of that stuff!"
She took the cigarette and contemplated putting it to
her lips and pretending to smoke it, when the phrase
about assertiveness popped into her mind. "The best
way not to get what you don't want is to say no to it."
She smiled at Haines. "No thanks," she said, passing the
cigarette to Dolores on her right, "I don't smoke grass."

Haines grinned and shrugged his shoulders. "We
each choose our own poison, I guess," he said, nodding
to the glass of wine in her hand.

"Britt's a dental hygienist," Dolores said brightly, to
no one in particular. Britt smiled to herself. Dolores was
obviously trying to draw her out, the way she used to
do in college. Well, it wasn't surprising, she knew, since
she had used Dolores as her social protector.

"Hey, Britt," said Dick, "I saw a kid today on the
outpatient pediatrics service who's had a low-grade in-
fection for months, and nobody figured it out. I examined him and found that his teeth were rotting out of

his head. If your practice handles kids, I'd like to refer him."

"Sure," Britt said, handing him a card, "we'd be glad to see him." She finished her wine, and discovered it was nearly one o'clock. "Hey, my friend," she said, putting an arm around Dolores's shoulders, "I've really had a lovely time, but I'd better be moving on. I'd like you to call me for lunch as soon as you can, okay?"

"You bet," said Dolores as they walked to the door, "and if I haven't called you in a week, you call me and lean on me a little, okay?"

"Fair enough," said Britt. With a wave to the group around the fire, and a final hug for Dolores, she departed.

Driving home, Britt pondered what seemed to her to be a small miracle. By altering her behavior she had talked with a group of people, made a tentative date with a guy, made a luncheon date with Dolores, received a referral patient. And she'd actually enjoyed herself! Maybe soon she'd even have to stop thinking of herself as shy.

You have a choice. Either of these two accounts can be yours. The first requires that you do nothing differently from what you have always done. Its results are continued isolation, loneliness, and negative feelings about yourself.

The second choice involves time, practice, and learning. But the results are contact, friendship, and positive feelings about yourself.

Which will you choose?

# Appendix:
# Relaxation Techniques

THE TWO EXERCISES that follow are designed to put you in a frame of mind that is open, relaxed, and ready to absorb the kinds of new thoughts about yourself that are presented in this book. For best results, record one or both of these exercises on a cassette tape recorder in a slow, relaxed tone. Then use them to get yourself relaxed before you use any of the tapes you have made specifically for yourself. You will find that the deepest relaxation is obtained in a dark, quiet room, with no one else present and no time deadlines to meet.

I. *Progressive Relaxation* (pause ten seconds for each series of ellipses [. . .])
Think for a few moments about your breathing . . . Notice how you draw each breath in and then let it out . . . Notice now what happens if you don't try to breathe —it just takes care of itself . . . So much of life is spent in working at things that just take care of themselves . . . If I just let it happen, my breath flows in, flows out, flows in, flows out, like the tides of the sea . . . I have nothing to do but relax . . .

Now I think of my toes . . . When I am tense and anxious, I clench my toes, but now I relax them completely, just letting go of them . . . It feels so good to relax . . . As my toes relax, a warm and comfortable feeling spreads from them through my feet, so that all of the tiny muscles in my feet relax and let go . . . I am becoming warm and comfortable . . . Now I loosen my ankles, I can feel that sense of warmth and comfort spreading from my feet into my calves . . . Those big muscles in my calves just become limp, so that my legs feel weak as a kitten's legs . . . I am warm and comfortable. Now I loosen all of the muscles in my thighs . . . the big muscles on the tops of my thighs . . . the muscles on the insides of my thighs . . . and the muscles on the back of my thighs . . . Now my legs feel very heavy . . . so heavy it would take a major effort to move them . . . My legs are as limp and limber as the legs of a rag doll . . . I am warm and comfortable . . . Now I let go of all tension in my buttocks . . . At the same time, my abdomen relaxes, so that I suddenly feel like I've taken off a tight pair of pants . . . I'm much more comfortable now . . . I feel like yawning or sighing . . . (pause) . . . When I do, I sigh out all the tightness of my chest. My breathing is now very quiet, and my chest hardly moves at all . . . Now I can feel the loosening of my back muscles, and as they loosen I can feel my back sink into the chair or bed . . . I feel so relaxed . . . My shoulders drop and loosen . . . My arms feel relaxed and heavy . . . I could lift them if I tried, but they're so heavy . . . Now the muscles of my neck just . . . let . . . go . . . and my head comes to rest in its most natural position . . . All of the tiny muscles in my face relax

. . . My cheeks sag . . . My mouth feels as if it wants to drop open . . . My eyes are closed and the lids feel very heavy . . .

While my body is very relaxed, my mind is open and alive and focused . . . I am concentrated only on the thoughts I have chosen to think . . . I am ready . . . I am at peace . . . I am relaxed and comfortable . . . I am warm and comfortable . . .

II. *Guided Imagery* (pause ten seconds for each series of ellipses [. . .])

I am relaxed and comfortable . . . I let my entire body come to rest and at peace . . . I close my eyes and enjoy the sense of restful floating . . . I listen to the sound of my breathing, deep and regular . . . I feel a light tingle in my hands and feet . . . I can sense my heartbeat and I can feel my pulse, slow and steady, as I lie comfortable . . .

I am going to a special place, a place that I know well . . . a place of peace and tranquility . . . a place where all is quiet, and I am quiet, and at rest . . .

NOTE:    IF YOU WISH, YOU MAY SUBSTITUTE YOUR OWN DESCRIPTION OF A PLACE THAT SEEMS VERY PEACEFUL TO YOU. IF NOT, USE THE DESCRIPTION THAT FOLLOWS:

It is a very warm, delightful summer day. I am standing beside a rapidly flowing creek. It is warm and there is very little wind and I am somewhat tired. The grass is green, the water is cool and refreshing, but I would like to get some breeze. Around me there are rolling hills covered with shade trees. I hear the song of the birds in the air. I see a hawk soaring overhead. I can hear the crickets singing and chirping. I am feeling so good that the warm sun makes me somewhat sleepy.

I relax deeper and deeper. I see myself beginning to climb the hill. As I climb the hill, I see the wild flowers as they are being rippled by the slight wind that comes up out of the valley. There is a smell of freshness in the air and the clouds overhead are racing along and they are slightly billowing. The sky around the clouds is azure blue. Everything is green and blue and fresh and clean. There is a goodness to the air. And as I walk up the hill I become more and more tired. It is difficult for me to put one foot in front of the other, but I have my eye on a large, shady oak tree at the top of the hill.

A tree that sends its shade out. A tree that I know will be in the best breeze. A tree that I know has been there for centuries. And it has grown strong because it has grown slowly. As I take in all the loveliness, I climb the hill. I can look around now to the distant scenery, the beautiful landscape. I see the mountains begin to form in the very far distance. They're slightly purplish. And as I climb up and up and up and up I am becoming more and more tired, more and more tired, but I keep climbing because it is so beautiful. I just want to get to the top. And as I go up and up I get more and more lethargic. I am feeling lazy like this warm, wonderful summery day. On top of the hill there are daisies and buttercups and many different wild flowers. There is a smell of new-cut hay coming across on the wind. There is a magnificently beautiful scene. And now I am at the top of the hill, and I am standing with my arms outstretched, letting the wind cool me. And as I am cooled by the wind, I go under the shade of the oak tree and sit down, so tired, feeling so good. I sit under this tree and as I sit under the tree I sink into a state of lethargy, not asleep, not awake. I let myself daydream and I daydream the most wonderful dreams, and I go deeper and deeper and deeper and deeper, just feeling so relaxed, feeling so good, feeling the warmth of the sun, feeling the freshness of the breeze, feeling the newness of the world. Just feeling so completely and totally relaxed.

Now, while I'm relaxed, I will let myself daydream about what it will be like when my problem, the problem on which I've been working, is totally and completely corrected. I will daydream about what it will be like when my problem is totally and completely corrected. Imagine how I will feel when I have changed my life so that my problem is not a part of my life. Imagine how I will feel when I have changed my life so that my problem is no longer a part of my life. What will be different about me and my life? What *will* be different about me and my life? I will daydream about how my behavior will be different. I will think about it. How will my behavior be different? I will daydream about how others in my life will feel and act differently toward me. I will imagine how others in my life will feel and act differently toward me.

The more I imagine how things *will be* when I have changed my life to the way I want it, the closer I come to making those changes. And the more I make those changes, the more I can imagine how things will be for me. The more I imagine how things will be when I have changed my life to the way I want it, the closer I come to making those changes, and the more I make those changes the more I can imagine how things will be for me. The more I imagine how things will be when I have changed my life to the way I want it, the closer I come to making those changes, and the more I make those changes the more I can imagine how things will be for me.

Now in the moment of silence that follows, I imagine some more, daydream some more about how good and how different things will be when I have made all the changes in my life that I have set out to make. Relax and imagine. . . .

# Index